What is Epistemology?

Polity's *What is Philosophy?* series

Sparkling introductions to the key topics in philosophy, written with zero jargon by leading philosophers.

Stephen Hetherington, *What is Epistemology?*
Charles Taliaferro, *What is Philosophy of Religion?*

What is Epistemology?

Stephen Hetherington

polity

The right of Stephen Hetherington to be identified as Author of this Work has been asserted in accordance with the UK Copyright, Designs and Patents Act 1988.

First published in 2019 by Polity Press

Polity Press
65 Bridge Street
Cambridge CB2 1UR, UK

Polity Press
101 Station Landing
Suite 300
Medford, MA 02155, USA

ISBN-13: 978-1-5095-2950-6
ISBN-13: 978-1-5095-2951-3(pb)

A catalogue record for this book is available from the British Library.

Library of Congress Cataloging-in-Publication Data

Names: Hetherington, Stephen Cade, author.
Title: What is epistemology? / Stephen Hetherington.
Description: Medford, MA : Polity, 2019. | Series: What is philosophy? | Includes bibliographical references and index.
Identifiers: LCCN 2018043384 (print) | LCCN 2018047897 (ebook) | ISBN 9781509529537 (Epub) | ISBN 9781509529506 (hardback) | ISBN 9781509529513 (pbk.)
Subjects: LCSH: Knowledge, Theory of.
Classification: LCC BD161 (ebook) | LCC BD161 .H46 2019 (print) | DDC 121–dc23
LC record available at https://lccn.loc.gov/2018043384

Typeset in 11 on 13 pt Sabon by Toppan Best-set Premedia Limited
Printed and bound in Great Britain by CPI Group (UK) Ltd, Croydon

For further information on Polity, visit our website: politybooks.com

Contents

Preface and Acknowledgements

There is philosophy within each of us.

'No, that's not me at all. I'm not philosophical.'

Actually, I'll bet that you are more philosophical than you realize. Do you think of yourself as lacking time or aptitude for philosophy? Have you ever really tried it? Have you ever taken it seriously?

'No, I've always had so much else to do. And no one encouraged me to think about philosophy.'

Well, *I'm* encouraging you, right now.

'Thanks. Okay, you say that I already have some philosophy within me. Why wouldn't I have noticed it? Surely it's impossible to have it without noticing it.'

No, it *is* possible. Even if you aren't conscious of an inner philosophy, it could be there, a part of you. Maybe others notice it, when watching how you behave: you might unwittingly be enacting a philosophy, displaying it in how you act, in how you carry yourself. Words are not always needed for this; you could be wordlessly living a philosophy. For example, perhaps you react sympathetically, respectfully, and generously to everyone, including people with a lower socioeconomic standing than your own. You might never notice this about yourself; you do it automatically. Even so, you would be *living* an acceptance of a form of egalitarianism – a thesis often discussed within political or social philosophy.

Of course, it is one thing to have a philosophy. It is another thing to have or live a *good* philosophy – one of which to be proud, with which you are content to be identified publicly. Is your philosophy already as good as it could be? As it should be? Those questions arise equally about a lived philosophy: what if you are only egalitarian in your actions within your own country, not when visiting elsewhere? Those are blunt questions, but we may react optimistically, seeing within them the invigorating idea of finding *and then improving* your philosophy. Nor does the optimism stop there: to improve your philosophy is to improve your *self*, particularly if your philosophy is located so deeply within you as to be animating and guiding your actions.

This book embraces that general theme, with a specific focus. We will be doing epistemology, a pivotal part of philosophy. Epistemology asks about the nature and value of *knowledge* – your knowledge, anyone's knowledge. And yes, you already have some epistemology within you. Believe me, you do. (Even being able and willing to think about this idea could mark you as somewhat epistemological.) Maybe yours is still a fledgling epistemology – fragmentary, incomplete, underdeveloped. It probably needs further work before it is polished, purposeful, powerful. How should you begin that work? How should you pursue it?

Here is how you can start: read this book, critically and questioningly. You will be reflecting deliberately and overtly upon philosophical ideas about knowledge. This will give you a better sense of what to look for in an epistemology. Otherwise, you might not understand even what thoughts within you, and what actions you perform, amount to an epistemology at all. You could be looking within yourself without adequate guidance. You might flounder. You might waste time and energy. You might lose motivation.

This book can fix all of that. It can help you to appreciate what an epistemology is. Feel encouraged to find your own epistemology. Then challenge yourself to enrich it. In that way, this is a self-help book. After reading the book, you will have more – and improved – epistemology within you. You will have thought further about what knowledge is and why it matters. You will have reflected upon this vital aspect of yourself.

Here is an analogy. It is likely that everyone has within them some moral philosophy, such as views about what makes an action or a person morally good or bad. But maybe not everyone has an *impressive* moral philosophy. As social media make abundantly clear, day after day, so many people have much to say about what is moral, and what is not. With unending energy, they express opinions on what is right and what is wrong – yet usually without depth and consistency, subtlety or complexity, in their moral stances. This could be improved by those people reflecting more philosophically upon morality – consciously noticing, modifying, and extending their own moral ideas, first of all. It *is* possible to become a better thinker, a more sage adviser, about moral matters.

And what is possible in that way for ideas about morality is also possible for ideas about knowing. This book is here to help you to sharpen and deepen your thinking about knowledge – what it is, what is involved in having it. This can be intellectually and personally demanding. Luckily, it is also fun.

Pascal Porcheron at Polity invited me to write this book. I welcomed the chance to do so. I enjoy the challenge of conveying complex philosophical ideas simply. (So I have minimized references, throughout the body of the book, to specific authors. Such details appear in the 'Further Reading' section.) Pascal gave me some very useful editorial advice, as did two anonymous referees. I am also grateful to Parveen Seehra for her helpful questions and comments on a draft of the book, and to Lindsay Yeates for his expertise regarding one of my examples.

1

Doing Epistemology

1.1 A parable, or two

What is epistemology? It is ... no, wait a moment. Let us start more slowly and reflectively, with an analogy.

Have you heard the parable of the blind men and the elephant? These men encounter their first elephant. 'What *is* this?' 'It's an elephant, I was told.' 'What is *that*?' One man – touching the trunk – answers that an elephant is like a snake. Another grasps an ear: 'An elephant is like a fan.' A third man feels the animal's side: 'No, an elephant is like a wall.' And so on. Each man touches a distinct part of the animal, deriving a view of the whole on the basis of that part – with each being mistaken about that whole. None of the men experiences enough of the elephant to know its general nature. But none of them thinks of himself as being too limited in that way. Each pronounces confidently – although ignorantly – upon the nature of elephants, by applying some evidence; not *enough* evidence, though.

We can adapt that parable. We can apply it to people puzzled about the nature of knowledge (rather than of elephants). We should do this because *epistemology* typically begins by reaching out and asking – puzzled – about knowledge's nature, as those blind men pondered the nature of elephants. How do we ensure that we will not fail as those men did? *Can* we understand knowledge's nature? Or – like the blind men – are we too restricted to do so? Must we remain ignorant, without realizing it, about what knowledge is?

Imagine asking different people, '*What* is knowledge?' This is not the same question as 'What is *known*?' In epistemology, our aim is not to compile a list of instances of knowledge – what you know, what your mother knows, etc. Such a list could include useful data, as we seek to understand what knowledge is. But it is not our ultimate goal. Instead, we want to push our thinking beyond any such list. We wish to discover what *makes* anything on that list an instance of knowledge: *why* is your knowledge knowledge? What makes *anyone's* knowledge knowledge? Thinking about only your knowledge, say, is like touching simply the elephant's tail. Thinking just about your mother's knowledge is like touching merely the elephant's tusk. We need to think far more widely about knowledge.

How much more widely, though? Knowing knowledge's nature is like knowing the nature of elephants. You need to observe or think about *enough* instances and aspects of knowledge, if you are to understand knowledge's nature, just as scientists need to observe or think about *enough* instances and aspects of elephants, if they are to uncover the general nature of elephants.

People usually assume that they use the term 'know' accurately because they already understand what knowledge is. But might that optimism be mistaken? Centuries of philosophical thought have discovered subtlety and complexity in the term 'know' (and its variants). Is everyone *aware* of that history, that subtlety and complexity? Imagine asking 'What is knowledge?' to people from different professions – educated people who are paid well to apply knowledge appropriate to their profession. Their answers could vary dramatically – so that not all of them could be correct – much as the blind men's answers did. A business-person might claim that all real knowledge ('worthy of the name') can be 'monetized' – usable in ways that bring financial success. A theoretical physicist might expect that all knowledge ('worthy of the name') encodes a numerical reality, regardless of whether money can be made from that knowledge. An experimental physicist might regard as real knowledge ('worthy of the name') only what can be verified by observations, including in controlled experiments. A sociologist might insist that all knowledge ('worthy of the name') is whatever is socially believed. And so on. Each professional gives voice to a conception of knowledge used within her field. Equally, though, maybe none of those professionals takes into account how the others – within *their* fields – think about knowledge's nature. Potentially, we have another version of the blind-men-and-the-elephant parable. Maybe each professional notices only part of the story, just an aspect of what knowledge is. Each might be wrong – too limited in their thinking – about knowledge in *general*.

That is more significant for them than they might realize. If you do not understand what knowledge in general is, you do not understand what knowledge is *at all*. Just as the blind men were wrong about what *even one* elephant is, each of our professionals might be wrong about what *even one* instance of knowledge is. That is, they could be wrong about what they assume is their *own* kind of knowledge, given their lack of understanding of knowledge in general. And none of them will notice this failing, just as each blind man was oblivious to his own failing.

This is where epistemology enters. It asks about knowledge in general – everyone's knowledge, all knowledge, at any time, in any place. It aims to reveal the nature of something – knowledge-possession – that could well unite us with people from all cultures and all centuries. *What* you know differs from what ancient Chinese or Greek people knew. Yet was their knowledge *the same general kind* of thing as yours? Knowledge seems to be something that people have long gained, especially as humanity has developed over the millennia. But can we be more detailed and insightful about *what* knowledge is?

With that question, we take a first step towards being epistemological.

1.2 Epistemology as philosophy

Further steps are then needed. After asking 'What is knowledge?', what should we do next? Well, epistemology is part of *philosophy*. Its methods and aims are philosophical. It seeks to understand knowledge *in a philosophical way*. But what does this mean? What is a philosophical understanding?

Here is a suggestion.

When someone claims to have a philosophy, for her it is a *template* and a *tool*. She uses it to regard, interpret, and react to the world – hoping to understand the world in a special way. What does 'special' mean here? Her philosophy is a *lens* through which she views the world, perhaps explaining to herself what she sees and experiences. Her philosophy can be a *manual* to guide her actions. She might be able to use it, often and widely: no matter what challenges she meets in life, she might hope that her philosophy will supply answers. It can also give her confidence about how best to describe and respond to the world.

Now, if that is the basic idea of a philosophy at all, many people should claim to have a philosophy. Many embrace a religion; and religions are often held in that same spirit, amounting to philosophies. If a philosophy is an *interpretive and motivating model* – helping one to regard and react to the world – then a religion can be a philosophy. Of course, not only religions are like that. An epistemology is a philosophy by being an interpretive and motivating model: it allows one to decide when knowledge is present, perhaps how to gain and act with knowledge. A religion can also be a philosophy by being an interpretive and motivating model, such as of the world's creation and of what it is to live morally well.

It seems, then, that there are many philosophies. But are all of them equally worthy, powerful, or insightful? Possibly not. One way for a philosophy to be better as a philosophy is for it to be a more *fundamental* picture of the world. There are at least the following two elements in this fundamentality.

First, a philosophy of X should portray X's fundamental *nature*. Religions often aspire to that, as do the epistemological theories that you will meet in this book. A religion wants to distinguish properly between whatever is sacred, say, and whatever is not – as part of understanding *what it is* to be sacred. An epistemology wants to distinguish properly between whatever is knowledge, say, and whatever is not – as part of understanding *what it is* to be knowledge. (The blind men needed – but failed – to distinguish properly between elephants and non-elephants, in trying to understand *what it is* to be an elephant.)

Second, a philosophy can portray a more, or a less, fundamental kind of *thing*, relative to reality as a whole. A religion, as a philosophy of the sacred, is a more fundamental philosophy of the ultimate nature of reality, say, than a philosophy of partying would be. The same is true of an epistemology, as a philosophy of knowledge. Parties can be fun. Presumably, though, the sacred and knowledge are more fundamental to reality – more ultimately definitional of reality and its potential – than parties are.

Still, *how* fundamental can an epistemology be? *How* deeply must we delve, into the world and ourselves, if we are to understand what it is to know?

1.3 Being epistemological

This book will try to help you to answer that question. First, though, here is a useful distinction: *having* a philosophy of X is not the same as *being philosophical* about X. The latter is active; the former need not be. One might possess a philosophy of X without doing anything philosophical with it. It is one thing to *have* an epistemology (a philosophy of X, for 'X' = 'knowledge'); it is another thing to *be* epistemological, even for a moment. And this book is mainly about being epistemological. It aims to be doing epistemology. It aims to encourage you to do epistemology.

A related distinction is between *an epistemology* and *being epistemological*. One can *be* epistemological with *an* epistemology. But this is not guaranteed: one could *have* an epistemology without *being* epistemological with it. An epistemology is a collection of theses or beliefs (like any other philosophy). Imagine someone, Rasa, waking from a long slumber, never having thought about philosophy, yet now having an epistemology in mind. The epistemology is Just There – suddenly, with no warning – in her mind. So, Rasa now *has* an epistemology. She writes it down, as its claims float through her consciousness. A friend says, 'That's an epistemology! From where did it come?' Rasa has no answer. She stares at those sentences, perplexed. How is she to use this epistemology, now present within her? Is it, for her, a useless bunch of thoughts, jostling pointlessly within her mind (no matter that they are epistemological in themselves, in their content)?

Actually, she could do much with those thoughts – not all of which amounts to being epistemological, though. Rasa might stand on a street corner, shouting her newly acquired epistemology at strangers; she might write its claims on pieces of paper, stick these on her bedroom walls, and repeat the claims to herself each morning, telling herself to believe them; etc. But none of this would be an epistemological *use* of these ideas. Yes, Rasa now possesses an epistemology, in a minimal way – as one can hold in one's hand a philosophy book, newly purchased. Yet one might never read and apply that philosophy book within one's life. Rasa possesses her epistemology like that, in literally a useless way. She does not own it in a way that will lead to her *being* epistemological in how she behaves: she will never *do* any epistemology with it.

What *would* be an epistemological way to act? Imagine being in a situation like Rasa's. For example, your philosophy teacher tells you to write down a bunch of sentences, telling you that these are from epistemology. How can you react epistemologically? How can you now be epistemological with those sentences?

You might begin by asking yourself whether they are true. Take the time to examine them critically – refining, testing, discarding, extending, replacing, etc. This might place in your mind a polished epistemology, one that 'feels true'. Is this all that is needed? For that moment, perhaps so. But if you then proceed to repeat the sentences mindlessly when asked about them (perhaps you believe them to be true), no longer are you being actively epistemological with them! So, continuing to be epistemological – even with that polished epistemology (those sentences, those claims) – is more than this. It includes remaining open actively to *continuing* to ask whether the philosophy in one's mind or hand is true: 'Although I think that it is true, might it be false? Are there good reasons to discard it, reasons that I have overlooked so far, reasons to replace it with a better philosophy?' Thinking like that is how one *lives* in being philosophical. So, in being actively epistemological, one is developing and examining ideas about knowledge, wondering genuinely whether the ideas (even while seeming true) might be false. (A perfect God, I take it, could have an epistemology. Presumably, this would be an ultimate epistemology, wholly true and complete. But surely God would never be *doing* epistemology, in the sense described here. God would never need to wonder whether His epistemology is true. He would not be like us in this respect, I assume.)

So, being epistemological can be intellectually demanding (because being philosophical can be like that). It can also be emotionally demanding. Courage might be needed: many people are scared to question a 'big' philosophy, let alone to discard one. I said that a religion can be a philosophy. To be religious, though, is not necessarily to be philosophical. If one is to be philosophical with one's religion, then one must be *genuinely questioning* it. This can be emotionally confronting, since one is raising a real possibility of losing one's religion.

It can likewise be emotionally confronting to question one's epistemology. 'Maybe I've been living with what I thought was knowledge – but really is not! Have I been so deluded about myself?' To take seriously this possibility – not treating it as a mere intellectual curiosity – is potentially unsettling. *Really* to wonder whether one has been so self-deluded? *Really* to wonder how to think and study, if one is to gain knowledge? *Really* to wonder how to evaluate one's cognitive, intellectual, professional, or educative efforts?

Certainly it is easy *not* to confront oneself in that way. It is easy to close one's mind to such awkward possibilities. Imagine being presented with an epistemology, perhaps in an engrossing book. The epistemology might include claims about knowledge's nature. What if you simply accept those claims, never really questioning their being true? You might then use the book as a manual, to decide whether various beliefs or opinions – yours or other people's – are knowledge. Time after time, you will say or think, 'Yes/no. My/your belief does/doesn't fit my conception of knowledge. So, it is/isn't knowledge.' You do this repeatedly, always brandishing the book, never refining or doubting its conception of knowledge. Is this how you want to be? You would be like someone who continually decides, in virtue of holding a 'fixed' conception of morality, whether various actions are morally good – without ever seriously wondering and questioning whether that conception of moral goodness is correct. Although that person *has* in mind a moral philosophy, she is not *being* philosophical with it. She is using her philosophy *dogmatically* – which is not a truly philosophical way to use it. She is never really *wondering whether* it is the right tool for the job of deciding which views are knowledge.

All of this gives us a simple moral: active questioning is needed for being epistemological, and then for staying epistemological. Of course, I am not advising anyone to become relentlessly epistemological by pondering knowledge's nature at every moment. But there are times to adopt an epistemological way of being. For instance, reflecting on knowledge's nature might alert you (as Chapter 3 will do) to the role of *good evidence* in having knowledge. This can make you better at using evidence, hence at gaining knowledge.

1.4 What epistemology is not

We have noted some features that epistemology shares with religion – but also how being epistemological seems to clash with being religious.

Or could we blend these two ways of being, in a religious epistemology? A simple first attempt to do so might give us this: 'Something is knowledge just in virtue of *God's deeming it* to be knowledge.' This is epistemological in its content, since it is about knowledge's fundamental nature. Yet one is not being epistemological in proposing this view about knowledge, unless one is genuinely prepared to examine, in an open-minded way, whether the claim is true in its linking of knowing and God. By all means, defend the claim as true. But if your defence is to be epistemological, you must really be inquiring into whether the claim is true. You must not merely be defending it against objections without really listening for whatever merit those objections might have. So, details of attitude and action matter for whether epistemology is actually being done.

It is easy to confuse epistemology with other areas of thought. For instance, epistemology is not a form of sociology. Imagine having a sociological description of some society as including widespread acceptance of various beliefs. These beliefs might play historically valued roles for those people. Still, this does not tell us whether those beliefs are knowledge: even a socially valued belief might not be knowledge. (And *calling* such beliefs 'knowledges' – as sometimes occurs in sociological discussions – reveals nothing constructive about knowledge's nature.) It is a further epistemological question whether that culturally significant pedigree makes a belief knowledge. Epistemologists ask whether the belief is likely to be *true*, or whether it is supported by genuinely good *evidence*. People's having a belief, even holding it passionately, need not make it true, or well supported by evidence, let alone knowledge: a group of people can be mistaken or irrational. Even a belief's having *long* been socially valued by many people does not guarantee its being knowledge: mistakes and irrationality can linger.

What of epistemology's relation to psychology? Suppose that we have a scientific description of how people, with their inherent cognitive structuring, tend to reason in forming some kinds of belief. The epistemological question then arises of whether people *should* reason in those ways, if knowledge is the aim. Some epistemologists consult psychological evidence about how people in general reason, in thinking about whether the beliefs being formed are knowledge: 'Are the beliefs being reached via *good* reasoning?' But is psychology the final word here? It has this possible advantage over sociology: maybe it uncovers 'hard-wired' facts about us, while sociology describes comparatively arbitrary aspects of how people form beliefs. Even psychology, however, might not be enough to tell us what it takes for reasoning to be *good* – that is, good enough to be producing knowledge.

1.5 Looking behind appearances

Suppose that being epistemological includes inquiring in a way that involves questioning, as it tries to decide between competing ideas about knowing's fundamental nature. How far should this questioning take us? Here we may reach for another important distinction, between what philosophers call *the manifest image* and *the scientific image*.

You have a choice as to how to be looking at the world. First, you can view it in an 'everyday' way – settling for the *manifest* image. You might think about the world in everyday terms, describing it in ways available to anyone, including people who have not learnt much science. Or, second, you could be seeing the world more as science does. You might describe the world by using scientific concepts and principles. Science lets you 'step behind' everyday appearances. Science lets you 'look behind' the manifest image, seeing something more fundamental, something deeper about reality. Science opens the door to the *scientific* image of the world.

Yet not all of our important thinking is either completely everyday or wholly scientific. There are 'in-between' options. For example, images that are less deep and powerful – but that are still *like* scientific insights into reality – are provided by plumbers, electricians, etc., when they reveal inner structural details of how houses are built and maintained. Otherwise, one would be limited to gazing upon a house in an everyday way, perhaps seeing it simply as strong, solid, sleek. That would be the house's *manifest* image. In contrast, what we can call an *artisan's* image of the house (extending the idea of a *scientific* image) can reveal something more vulnerable, more fragile, with lots of potential – hidden from the less informed gaze of a prospective purchaser – for problems to arise within the house's inner or deeper aspects. The artisan's image understands better the house's underlying reality, and its fundamental details, than are revealed by the manifest image of the house (the mere *dweller's* image?).

That sort of added insight is also akin to what we gain through what could be called *the philosophical image* – including *the epistemological image*. People talk casually of what seems to be knowledge, of who knows what. Is it really knowledge, though? Even if various claims or beliefs look like knowledge when viewed in everyday ways or settings – within a *manifest* (non-philosophical) image of the world of knowing – maybe a longer and more searching perusal behind that appearance reveals something more complicated, even something quite different. This deeper look behind that appearance is what we gain by doing epistemology, seeking an *epistemological* image of the world of knowing.

The result could be like a kind of experience that I have been having recently in Sydney. Many buses these days have large advertisements on their exterior, spread across the windows (able to be removed, new ones taking their place). From outside the bus, one sees a glamorously portrayed Hollywood actor, for instance. From inside the bus, one gazes through those same windows – experiencing the passing world, in not quite a normal way, through what is actually a mosaic of tiny holes, noticeable with a shift of attention, separated from each other with a pattern of lines. This is the inner reality, as it were, of what has been attached to the bus – but of what, when viewed from outside, looks like the Hollywood actor. From outside, one sees the apparent reality as it is designed to be seen: a glamourous picture. From inside, one sees the same reality differently. One sees it from behind, noticing how the outer effect is created. Well, doing epistemology – forming an epistemological image – is like entering the bus, remembering how it looks from outside, while now seeing it from inside – yet also now understanding how that outside appearance is created. Doing epistemology is complex. Welcome aboard!

1.6 This book (and a hint of history)

The term 'epistemology' did not enter the English language until the nineteenth century. But epistemological thinking is much older than that. The term 'epistemology' comes from the ancient Greek word '*epistēmē*', usually translated as 'knowledge'. So, epistemology is the 'ology' of knowledge, the 'theory' of knowledge. It is 'knowledge*ology*' (to introduce an ungainly term!), and hence epistemologists are 'knowledge*ologists*'! The first written epistemological thinking within Western philosophy comes from Plato, around the fourth century BCE in Athens, mainly in his *Meno* and his *Theaetetus*. Plato gave Western philosophy so much, not only epistemology. (What an amazing time and place to have lived! Socrates taught Plato, who then taught Aristotle. These are among the greatest philosophers ever.) Along with much else within philosophy, epistemology was under way.

Between then and now, epistemology's role within philosophy has shifted shape and location a number of times. It has always been there, in one form or another.

At times, it has been the most prominent and respected part of philosophy; at other times, it has played a supporting role, standing patiently in the background. In some centuries, its emphasis has been on describing *ways and kinds* of knowing. There have been periods when *doubts* about knowing have dominated, feeling like serious threats to our ever having knowledge. And, of course, what *is* knowledge in the first place? This question was posed by Plato, and has been vigorously debated in recent decades: can we definitively define *what knowledge really is*?

This book will discuss all of those main strands within the evolving history that has constituted epistemology over the past 2,500 years. (To be epistemological is thus to reflect, in a genuinely inquiring and philosophical way, on at least some of those strands.) Chapter 2 is on *ways and kinds* of knowing. Chapters 3 and 4 are on *what knowledge really is*. Chapter 5 is on *doubts* about knowing. Chapter 6 will gesture at how we might usefully – and provocatively – apply some of those questions and ideas within our lives.

2

Kinds of Knowledge

2.1 Data, please

Chapter 1 encouraged us to understand what it really is to have some knowledge. Chapter 3 will engage fully with that challenge. Before we can do so, though, we need *data* – knowledge-data. We also need to *organize* those data if we are to find a good theory (of knowledge's nature) with which to interpret them. All of that is this chapter's role: to gather knowledge-data; to start organizing the data; to notice whatever epistemological themes emerge.

This approach to inquiry should seem familiar. Before anyone could have understood what it is to be an elephant, for example, good elephant-data were needed. Over here: this is an elephant. Over there: it looks like ... yes, another elephant. Notice any shared features that might matter for classifying and understanding these animals. Observe the animals' behaviour – what they do, where and how they do it. Will this reveal why they act as they do? And look further afield, for a wide range of individuals. Down there: is that a group of them? Yes. Watch how it acts. Now find another group. And another. Continue looking. Collate these data. Then *think*. Theorize. Interpret. We have given these animals a name: 'elephant'; now embed that name within a theory of their nature. This theory of elephants – elephantology? – could include surprises, as science often does. In fact, science tells us that elephants are most closely related to hyraxes (a kind of herbivorous mammal), dugongs ('sea cows') and manatees (fresh-water versions of dugongs). *That* is surprising. And only with science – not mere casual observation – could we reach this surprising interpretation of elephants. We are gazing upon the *scientific* image – not the manifest image – of elephants. (Remember this form of distinction, from section 1.5.)

It could be useful to remember that example while reading this chapter. We are about to venture into the wild, gathering data – *knowledge*-data. The sweaty task awaits of gathering samples and recording observations: '*That* looks like knowledge. Note its details. Add it to the list.' Then the next chapter will return us to the comfort of our studies or offices, as we start interpreting the knowledge-data collected in this chapter. But our initial challenge is to search thoughtfully, finding and organizing instructive examples of knowledge. We will examine these for shared features and distinguishing marks. We will observe how these examples function – how they are used – as knowledge. There are different kinds of elephant, all of them sharing an underlying nature as elephants. Are there different kinds of knowledge, all of them sharing an underlying nature as knowledge? Some zoologists strive for a full theoretical picture of what it is to be an elephant. This is a challenge. Some philosophers – epistemologists – strive for a full theoretical picture of what it is to be knowledge. This is also a challenge.

2.2 Who or what knows?

As section 1.6 mentioned, Western epistemology began in ancient Greece, mainly with two of Plato's dialogues (*Meno* and *Theaetetus*). Chapter 3 will discuss some key epistemological ideas bequeathed by those dialogues. In the meantime, we should note something that will feel quite natural: Plato focused on what it is for an *individual person* to know something. This has continued to be epistemology's central concern; and so it will be ours. You might not expect it to be puzzling. But it is. First, though, let us notice a few *more obviously* puzzling possible cases of knowing.

2.2.1 Brains?

When we say that someone knows something, are we attributing knowledge only to the person *as a whole*? Or could a *part* of a person have knowledge? That sounds odd. But there is a way to make it sound less odd.

You know that you are alive, for instance. For argument's sake, suppose that this knowledge is somehow recorded in your brain, so that you – a person as a whole – have the knowledge. Should we also accord your *brain* that same knowledge? Perhaps your brain has the knowledge in a different way to how you-as-a-whole do. If so, there are at least those *two* knowers of that same truth – your brain and you! (Think of hypnotism, a less everyday example. Can it help a *person* to bring to awareness – now as an object of memory – a version of some knowledge that would otherwise have remained in her *brain* – 'imprinted' there earlier?)

2.2.2 Extended minds?

Quickly, tell me: what is the capital of Mongolia? You do not know? Perhaps you do – in the sense of being *able* very speedily to be conscious of it. Inside your pocket is your mobile phone, courtesy of which you can have the answer ('Ulaanbaatar') almost immediately. That phone is practically a part of you. Although it is not your brain, it functions like an *extension* of your brain.

Quickly again, tell me: what is the population of Benin? You do not know? Again, you are needlessly modest. Your phone is right there, comfortingly in your hand. You can consciously know the answer ('nearly 11.5 million', when I am writing this) within a minute. So, you do already *implicitly* have the knowledge – because the phone can provide the knowledge almost immediately, and because the phone may as well be treated as an extension of your brain, of your mind. You know, because the phone knows – and because the phone is practically a part of you.

That is an hypothesis, a possible interpretation. Like the picture from a moment ago, of your brain being a knower, this one requires us to think in a new way about who or what has knowledge.

2.2.3 The world?

Might some knowledge exist without being held by an individual thing (a person, a brain) at all?

Imagine a brain, containing some knowledge ('I am alive'), suddenly being *removed* from its surrounding body. Picture the brain being connected to a machine that allows it to function, staying alive even if no longer sensing the world (such as through eyes linked to it). Does the brain continue having that knowledge ('I am alive'), even while gaining no new knowledge?

Imagine, next, that you leave your phone at a shopping mall. It sits for a few hours, switched on, recharging, in a remote corner of the mall. When you wandered away distractedly, the phone was displaying the population of

Benin. We asked just now (section 2.2.2) whether the phone is a knower when in your hand. If it is, does it remain so, once on its own? Can the phone know even when *not* functioning as an extension (cradled in your hand) of your mind?

Imagine, third, that the world includes (in books and/ or online) information that will nevermore be read or brought to mind. To become aware of it would be to gain (personal) knowledge. Yet that will not happen for this information. Is all of this material knowledge, even so? Maybe some was knowledge in a more familiar way, a personal way, when initially formulated after related research. But that was then, and this is now: no one *remains* aware of the material.

We have imagined three puzzling cases. Each gestures at what could be called *unowned* knowledge. It would be *personally* unowned knowledge. But can we think of it as *the world's* knowledge – 'owned' by the world? It is not possessed by an individual knower, someone among us: it would be knowledge 'out there', independent of us. Following the lead of Karl Popper, a twentieth-century Austrian-British philosopher, it could be called *objective* knowledge. This is not a way of praising it. The point is that the knowledge lacks *subjective* existence, in the sense of being present in someone's mind, an object of actual thought. This kind of objective knowledge is in effect an object or artefact, present in public space. It is available to be *used* as knowledge (regardless of whether this will ever occur).

2.2.4 Groups?

Might some knowledge be owned, but not by individuals? Is knowledge ever owned by a *group* as a whole (without being owned by individuals within it)?

This could be a vital possibility. Where would societies be without science? Nowhere modern. Where would science be without group research? Nowhere modern. Picture the research for an article in a scientific journal being performed by thirty people across five universities in three countries. This is a realistic picture. Suppose – also realistically – that no single one of those thirty scientists had the expertise to fully understand all aspects of the research. Can the article be knowledge? If so, whose knowledge is it? Just the world's? Maybe – except that there are those thirty names attached to it. If knowledge has been produced by them, and is now possessed by the world, it is knowledge that no *single* one of those thirty scientists could have possessed or produced. The knowledge comes only from those people when working as members of a group – the entire group. Their work discovered a truth that would have been beyond their reach as individuals. Does only *the group* know that truth?

That question arises before the article is published. But even after publication, maybe no one among the thirty can fully understand and explain the article. Is it still only the group's knowledge? Imagine that (as in section 2.2.3) no one ever reads the published article. It rests in scientific oblivion. Is it then unowned knowledge – *group* unowned knowledge, in that only a group could ever own it, no matter that no future group does ever come to own it?

Sometimes, group knowledge is also individual knowledge. Picture a group of people watching a storm approaching. This group knowledge of the storm's progress is a function of the group's members sharing the knowledge: the group has the knowledge, *in that* the group's members do. Often, though, this is not quite so simple: a group can have some knowledge, because *enough* of its members have it. But how large a proportion of the group needs it, if the group itself is to have it? Can there be a general answer to that question? ('We in Australia know that ... .' Could this be true even when not everyone has the knowledge that ...? How would this happen?)

2.2.5 Animals?

Many people are convinced that their beloved pet dog or cat, say, has knowledge. Place a bowl of dog food in front of Rex. Watch him react. The word 'dinner' will not emerge from his mouth. But does he know that it is a meal for him? He will not know the situation as we know it. Might he know it in *some* terms, though? What of his good friend Tina, that bedraggled mutt from across the road? Does he know that she was here not long ago? We cannot say for sure that he does. Yet all of that sniffing by him seems to have some point; and don't we generally believe that it is knowledge – even a kind of inquiry – that guides Rex as he hurries from fence to post to wall, sniffing and raising his leg and …? Your own meagre human nostrils are useless in that respect. Rex is not only a knower, it seems; he would be the superior knower in this setting!

Is he also a different *kind* of knower? Or is there enough kinship between Rex's knowledge – animal knowledge (dog knowledge?) – and a person's knowledge? The kinship might not be in *what* is known ('dinner' versus however-Rex-conceives-of-the-meal). Nor might it be in how the knowledge is gathered (via your lesser nostrils versus Rex's superior ones). Even so, are you *enough* like Rex – in that you and he gain knowledge in what, considered more fundamentally, is a similar way? (And what might that similarity be? That question hurries us to the next section.)

2.3 How does knowledge arise?

2.3.1 Perception

You and Rex share this: each relies on sensing or perceiving, in striving to know the surroundings. Epistemologists have long sought to describe fundamental *ways* in which knowledge arises. The senses – looking, listening, sniffing, tasting, touching – seem to give us perceptual or observational knowledge. Philosophers have traditionally called this *a posteriori* knowledge. The idea behind that name is that observational knowledge is available only *as a result of, hence after* – or *posterior* to – observational experience of what is known.

One question then asks about *what* we perceive, when having perceptual knowledge. Does perception deliver 'pure' or 'basic' sensory data, from which we 'construct' knowledge of the world? In other words, is perception, strictly speaking, only of *uninterpreted* or 'raw' colours, shapes, smells, etc. – more basic elements of reality? Or is perception already *interpretive*, being of a house, a person, a drum solo, etc. – complex elements of reality? What do we observe? We say that we see a house. But is that loose talk, because really we see only colours and shapes – after which we use something more than sensing to 'construct' the idea that a house is what we see?

It is simpler to begin our epistemological efforts with the hypothesis that we see 'fuller' aspects of the world, such as a house, rather than only 'raw' colours and shapes. Treating perceptual data as uninterpreted (as 'raw' or 'immediate' interactions with 'basic' elements of reality) is already philosophically interpretive! Even if we should end by adopting that interpretation, it is probably wiser to *begin* with a more everyday hypothesis. This means our beginning with the manifest image (see section 1.5) that the world presents to us. We talk of perceiving a house, a person, a drum solo, etc. Let us begin by taking such talk at face value, working with that manifest image.

2.3.2 Reason

How else would you gain knowledge? 'I think!' You do indeed. But we can be more specific. You reason: call this *reasoning*. Maybe you also 'see' without literally seeing: call this *pure insight*. We now consider these in turn.

First, reasoning is active. It is inferential. It starts from premises, data, or evidence; it then infers to what seems to follow from, or to be well supported by, those premises, etc. If one *starts* from knowledge, reasoning can take one to *further* knowledge. This would be *inferential* knowledge.

Second, might your mind have a capacity for pure insight? This need not be inferential. Can timelessly true truths be revealed, perhaps effortlessly? For example, might reason reveal truths of pure mathematics ('2 + 2 = 4'); perhaps also of logic ('From *If A then B*, and *Yes, A*, it follows that *Yes, B*'); and perhaps some fundamental metaphysical truths? These metaphysical insights could range from the humdrum ('Nothing can be true and not true at once') to the reassuring ('For anything that exists, in principle there is an explanation of how it exists') – to the downright exciting ('God exists').

We saw that observational knowledge is traditionally called *a posteriori* knowledge. Any knowledge arising purely through reason – pure insight – is non-observational. Its traditional name is '*a priori* knowledge'. If such knowledge is possible, in theory it can arise *independently* of – *prior* to – observational experience of what is known. It might be knowledge of what cannot possibly be observed. Could you literally perceive the pure mathematical state of affairs that 2 + 2 = 4? Seemingly, no.

2.3.3 Memory

Here is a complication: sensing takes time, as does reasoning; even a flash of pure insight takes time. And during that period you might forget how it began. You could forget the data with which you began the

reasoning. Or you might not hold in mind the first stage
of your sensing an event, so that by the time it ends you
are seeing *only* the end of it, no longer knowing how it
started: even speedily observing a static object like a
house has an initial moment, an in-between period (even
if this is brief), and a final moment. When memory fails,
this affects your ability to have *any* knowledge.

There is also the simpler point that much of what
you claim to know even in an ordinary way depends
on your memory functioning well, linking you accurately to an earlier time. Do you know what movie
you watched yesterday? Only if you remember watching it. Do you know what your name is? Only if you
remember pertinent events from your life. Do you
know whether Germany was involved in World War
II? Only if you remember what you were taught about
this. And perhaps you *can* remember such things.
Memory seems like another fundamental way for
people to gain and maintain knowledge. (Maybe this
can happen both normally and abnormally. Do you
recall section 2.2.1's asking you about hypnosis? When
it helps to bring to awareness some specific knowledge,
is this now memory knowledge – even if gained in an
abnormal way?)

2.3.4 Testimony

Most of us would say that we know quite a lot about
World War II. Yet few of us observed any events in that
war, since we were not alive at the time. We listen now
to the words of others. We look at photographs. We
read or hear assessments by experts. We trust oral and
written histories by those who were involved. In all of
this, we rely on testimony – not always legal testimony,
but testimony in a wider sense. We rely on evidence that
ultimately is traceable back – via chains of assurance
and communication (testimonial chains) that we might

now be unable to describe – to observations by people who did observe World War II events.

Does that reliance give us (testimonial) knowledge of aspects of that war? This would require testimony to be a trustworthy method, able to *transmit* knowledge that might have arisen initially, for other people, in another way (such as through personal observation by those people). Others saw what was happening, gaining observational knowledge at the time; enough of their observations were recorded; enough of these have been preserved; you can now consult enough of those records – which amount to testimony, traceable to those people's observational knowledge, of what happened. An eye-witness observes Nazi atrocities; she writes about them; you read what she wrote. Do you thereby – through her written testimony – gain knowledge of those atrocities? This would be indirect knowledge.

Obviously, our lives should teach us that not all testimony is reliable or trustworthy: people do lie and misremember. Still, whenever testimony *is* reliable and trustworthy, can knowledge be the result?

2.3.5 Introspection

In thinking about ways to know, notice how important it can be to read one's own mind: *what* evidence is in there, courtesy of the sensing, the thinking, etc.? Imagine someone asking you how you know what America's foreign debt is. You have read an informative article on this. You remember doing so. You find yourself *bringing to your awareness* important details from the article. This process of bringing-to-one's-own-awareness is called *introspection*.

This need not involve being moody or self-absorbed, losing involvement with the social world. ('She is depressingly introspective!') The epistemological idea is that, while perception is of a world 'outside' one's mind, introspection is of what is 'inside' one's mind. For instance, introspection could be a way for you to know what data are in your mind, after using your senses. If you cannot introspect, your awareness is 'cut off' from what your senses are trying to tell you about the world. You will not know *what* evidence is coming from your senses; in which case, you will be unable to reason well *from* that sensory evidence to knowledge of the world. In short, introspection – your looking *within* your mind – might be needed by you, even for your perceptions to give you knowledge of a world *outside* your mind.

And do not forget knowledge of how you are *feeling*. This can be part of self-knowledge. Without such self-knowledge, you might not know much else. You might not know, for example, whether you are reading the world accurately, if you do not know your inner mood, and hence cannot know whether to 'correct for' its being a mood that is making you misjudge what is happening around you. (Being unhappy, say, could make you 'see' the world differently in many respects. But so could being happy: you might overlook others' suffering, for instance.)

2.3.6 *Common sense*

You might shrug your shoulders at all of this, reassuring yourself that common sense is always available: when thinking becomes abstruse, common sense remains a sturdy and knowledgeable friend. There are many moments, I expect, when your response to a question is the comforting 'It's common sense, isn't it? So, of course I know it.' *Is* common sense a way of gaining knowledge?

This depends on what common sense is. When you claim to be using it, is this a vague way of pointing to a claim (i) that you believe or assume would be shared by most other people, (ii) that you take to be knowledge, or close to it, and (iii) that you cannot explain in some other way as being knowledge? (If you could explain its being knowledge in terms of testimony, say, it would be knowledge from testimony, not from common sense.) Is common-sense knowledge some commonly shared but otherwise inexplicable knowledge?

We might attempt a tentative explication of the general idea, though. Is common sense like a less ambitious form of reason – in the sense of pure insight (section 2.3.2)? If pure insight can offer special insight into wonderful metaphysical truths, does common sense provide everyday – *not* special – insight into everyday – *not* special – truths? Is common sense a separate way of knowing, even in its ordinariness?

2.3.7 *Intuition*

Contemporary philosophers often claim to base a thesis on what they call 'intuition' or 'my intuitions'. On a good day, intuitive knowledge will be claimed: 'I know, intuitively, that this action/belief is wrong/knowledge.' That sounds promising, as we embark upon doing some epistemology. What, then, is intuition? Is it a further way of gaining knowledge?

Intuition is at least introspective (section 2.3.5): one looks within, asking how a particular idea or view strikes one. It is not claimed to be observational (section 2.3.1). It might be thought, by its philosophical fans, to come from reason – not always reasoning, but a flash of insight (section 2.3.2). If so, it should probably be trusted.

Another possibility is that what philosophers call 'intuition' is just a kind of common sense (section 2.3.6). Maybe it counts as common sense among philosophers when they are engaging with philosophical questions. I offer no definitive verdict on this; I invite you to monitor your own thinking, your own reactions, while reading this book. Will you rely on intuitions when evaluating the epistemological questions and ideas that you will meet? Would that be a strength – a path taken to gain epistemological knowledge? Or can it be a weakness, an intellectual dogmatism, an unwitting admission of not having much to say in defence of a given epistemological view? (In section 4.7 we will return to the issue of epistemology and intuitions, when discussing experimental philosophy.)

2.4 What forms does knowledge take?

We have been asking about *sources* of knowledge: in what distinctive ways do people form beliefs that are a correlative *kind* of knowledge? Perceptual knowledge would arise through perception, testimonial knowledge through testimony, intuitive knowledge through intuition, etc.

Now we should ask about possible *forms* that a piece of knowledge could have. No matter how it has been formed, a sculpture *looks* a particular way, having literally a specific form. We can look at pieces of knowledge in a similar way. This section shows what that means in practice. (We can also think of this section as about the *objects* of knowledge.)

Incidentally, this section's title asks about 'forms', not 'form', to leave open the possibility of there being different basic appearances that knowledge might take. We will now test that possibility.

2.4.1 Knowledge-that

Epistemological discussion of knowledge usually concerns what philosophers call 'knowledge-that'. We are about to examine several forms that this might take (before section 2.4.2 notes another possible knowledge-form). Here is the basic idea of knowledge-that (before the subsections that follow highlight specific forms within this general category of knowledge-that).

When philosophers talk of knowledge-that, they are referring to its having this form: 'So-and-so knows that ...'. In practice, the '...' is replaced by an indicative sentence or proposition (and the 'so-and-so' by someone's name, say). The indicative sentence replacing the '...' is supposed to describe a worldly detail being known: 'Fred knows that *he is drinking coffee*', 'Tina knows that *Fred drinks too much coffee*', 'Fred knows that *when he drinks coffee he has religious experiences*', etc. Does all knowledge take this form? Is all knowledge propositional – descriptive – in this way?

I will now highlight various ways to use the word 'knowledge' – in all of which, it seems, we are talking about a version of knowledge-that. A distinction between what Bertrand Russell famously called 'knowledge by description' and 'knowledge by acquaintance' will run throughout these examples.

2.4.1.1 Knowing who

I know *who* Donald Trump is. I know (while writing this) that he is the US President, having been a real estate tycoon and a reality TV host. So, I have propositional knowledge about him: I know these truths about him, these descriptions of him, through socially standard forms of testimony. I also know who he is through perception: I know what he looks like. Although I cannot describe him fully, I am visually acquainted with him: I could recognize him reliably in a police line-up. (This might involve knowledge-*how*, such as knowing how to respond when asked 'Which one is Donald Trump?')

2.4.1.2 Knowing a person

Although I know who Donald Trump is, I do not know *him*. I do not know him by having met him, being personally acquainted with him – having that sort of experience of him, knowing that *this person with whom I am speaking is Donald Trump*. I do know my wife in that sense: countless times, I have known that *this person with whom I am speaking is my wife*. So, the complexity in knowing a person involves having propositional knowledge – knowing truths about the person, knowing descriptions of her. (This might also include a recognitional capacity – again, some knowledge-how.)

2.4.1.3 Knowing a place

I know *Sydney* descriptively: I know many truths about it. Anyone who reads about Sydney can likewise know those truths – sharing that (descriptive) propositional knowledge with me. I also know Sydney, though, in that I have many Sydney-abilities based in my direct acquaintance with the city: I recognize much within it; I know how to travel around it.

2.4.1.4 Knowing when

I know *when* I was born. I know this descriptively, on the basis of testimony and perception. I know what my birth certificate says, and I know that it is a birth certificate, produced reliably. In all of this, mistakes are possible. Still, the kind of knowledge in question remains propositional – descriptive.

2.4.1.5 Knowing this rather than that

I know that Donald Trump is the US President *rather than* the Australian Prime Minister. I know that Donald Trump is the US President *rather than* the UK Prime Minister. And so on. Might (descriptive) propositional knowledge always take this form? Is knowledge always of some circumstance *as against another* circumstance? A *contrastivist* about knowledge says that knowledge is always like this. Knowledge would thus be of a specific truth only in a comparative or qualified way, not an absolute way. I would not know *simply that* Donald Trump is the US President. I would know only that he is US President *as against another* possible state of affairs, such as that he is a New York City subway driver. Often, when asking whether someone knows a specific circumstance, a questioner has in mind an alternative: 'Do you know that you are eating a salami sandwich?' – as against a pepperoni sandwich, not a salami and blueberry muffin, say. But even when a contrast like this is not in the questioner's mind, is there an *implicit* comparing or contrasting? Even this is propositional knowledge: it is knowledge-that, even if what follows the 'knows that' is more *complex* – having the form '... rather than ——' rather than just '...'.

2.4.1.6 Knowing a topic

I know much, in a descriptive way, about cricket. (I also know *how* to play it. For now, though, we are leaving to one side the nature of knowledge-how.) I know truths about the history, the rules and techniques. So, my knowledge of this *topic* includes many instances of descriptive knowledge, propositional knowledge. (This might also involve knowledge-how: I know how to move via reasoning between these truths, being familiar in traversing the domain of cricket truths.)

2.4.1.7 Knowing why

Sometimes, I know *why* a circumstance obtains, or an event happened. Is this because I know appropriate truths, such as background conditions and relevant general principles or laws? If so, once more we are in the company of descriptive knowledge, propositional knowledge.

2.4.1.8 Knowing what it is like

I know what it is like to be Australian, I think. But I definitely do not know what it is like to be the Prime

Minister of Australia. I know what it is like to play cricket; unfortunately, I do not know what it is like to have played cricket for Australia. There is knowing what it is like to *be* X; there is knowing what it is like to *do* Y. These (the 'X' and the 'Y') include experiences, observations, memories – which involve descriptive knowledge. But this knowledge is available only to someone who occupies a particular role or place, something that can occur more *or* less easily. (Everyone can accurately say, 'Unlike me, you do not know what it is like to be me.' Almost no one can accurately say, 'Unlike me, you do not know what it is like to be the Australian Prime Minister.')

2.4.2 *Knowing how*

Must we now venture away from that familiar neighbourhood where so much descriptive knowledge lives? Is knowledge-*how* a deeply different form of knowledge from propositional knowledge (knowledge-that, descriptive knowledge)?

Knowledge-how is knowledge *how to do* something. I have mentioned, in the past few subsections, recognitional capacities that might be involved in some kinds of knowledge-that; and such capacities can be conceived of as instances of knowledge-how. When I see a photograph of Donald Trump in front of the Empire State Building in New York City, I recognize it, enabling me to reply 'yes' to the question of whether he was in NYC yesterday. This reply is an *action* that I can perform, once I have this (recognitional) knowledge of Donald Trump, this (distant) acquaintance with him. I would have this knowledge-*how*. It is possible, then, that much knowing involves both knowledge-that *and* knowledge-how.

Initially, that makes our story about all of this more complex. But can we simplify it? Can we understand one of these forms of knowledge in terms of the other, so that there is really only one underlying kind of knowledge involved?

For example, when I know *how* to ride a bicycle, must this involve crucial knowledge-*that*? Could my knowing how to ride a bicycle be my knowing various truths about correct-riding-technique (even if I do not bring these truths to mind when riding the bicycle)? Might it include my knowing P, where P is some complex physics describing the movements of my body and the bicycle? Is all of *that* inside my mind, thanks to my knowing how to ride a bicycle? I recall a physicist suggesting that the famous English soccer (football) player David Beckham had implicit knowledge of the physics involved in knowing how to kick a ball to make it curve prodigiously in flight.

Alternatively, did Beckham's knowledge-how (skills) require no such knowledge-that? Could he have been excellent at kicking the ball, without having any special knowledge that S, where S is some complex physics describing the movements of his body and the ball?

Intellectualism is the thesis that any knowledge-how is ultimately knowledge-that. When I ride a bicycle, this is what epistemologists call an *intelligent action*: it exemplifies or manifests knowledge-how (my knowing how to ride a bicycle); it is not a merely random movement. Intellectualists say that I perform this action only by applying (even if unconsciously) knowledge-that, such as knowledge of truths from what we might call a *textbook* for how to ride a bicycle. Beckham, too, would be applying his knowledge that S. I mention intellectualism because many epistemologists regard it as a promising hypothesis that could simplify the challenge of understanding the fundamental nature of knowledge in general.

So, we will concentrate on knowledge-that (descriptive knowledge).

2.5 Next – a theory of knowledge

This has been a chapter of data-gathering and data-organizing. How do people use the word 'know'? What patterns are there in such uses? What themes emerge from all of this? We have been answering these questions. We are now ready to confront an ancient epistemological question: what *is* knowledge?

We may treat this as the question of what it is to have *propositional* knowledge – descriptive knowledge, knowledge-that. Chapter 5 will ask whether people *do* have knowledge. Before then, chapters 3 and 4 will create and shape a theory, a philosophical picture, of knowledge's fundamental nature – of what knowledge is, regardless of whether people do actually have some.

3

A First Theory of Knowledge

3.1 Some guiding principles

So, our immediate goal is clear: build a theory of knowledge! Find an interpretive model, a philosophical picture – an accurately insightful one. We need to understand how knowing differs from not knowing.

How can we accomplish that? One natural reply is this: 'I will just *think* about this. That will reveal to me *my* conception of knowledge. Then I'll ask others whether my conception matches theirs – what *they* take knowledge to be.'

But perhaps we should not trust simply to inspiration. Are there good principles of theory-building and theory-choice with which we might guide that inner exploration and social calibration? Here are a few possibilities.

1 We want a philosophical model or understanding of *all* knowledge. Chapter 2 described several types of knowledge. Even if they differ in details, does a *general pattern* unite them?

2 What *type* of pattern might that be? In general, philosophers have a choice between these forms of theory (for some phenomenon X):

- Try to understand X by 'breaking it down' analytically: treat X as a complex, with an 'inner structure'. What are X's fundamental *parts*?
- Try to understand X by describing its links (perhaps leaving aside its 'inner structure') within a larger network of phenomena. What are X's fundamental *roles*?

Epistemologists have tended to follow the first – the 'analytical' – path when trying to understand knowledge's nature. We will do likewise. (The other approach might emerge anyway.)

3 Will that 'analytical' way of understanding X succeed only if we can *independently* understand those 'parts' mentioned in our analysis of X? For instance, we could try to understand knowing's nature by describing components – A, B, C – that are blended within any instance of knowing, saying something like 'knowledge = A+B+C.' We would be confident of *already* understanding A, B, and C fairly well. Then we would aim to turn our understanding of A, B, and C into an understanding of knowledge.

4 In all of this, *how* good must our understanding be? How deep? How extensive? How fine-grained? It might be unhelpful to decide this in advance. Let us see what unfolds.

5 We want our theory to be as simple and elegant as possible. We want it to say enough – and no more. A good theory does not waste words.

6 We want our theory to notice relevant differences. It should tell us how to sort, how to demarcate, knowing from not knowing. Something is knowledge if it fits the theory – and not knowledge if it does not fit the theory.

So, here is the chapter's plan. Start – and end – with as simple a theory as possible. Add to the initial version in small steps, stopping once we reach what seems to be no more than is needed. (All of this will happen in the next few sections.) At each step along the way – while carefully constructing our theory, piece by piece, like a coral reef – our overarching question is this: 'Have we said enough? Or are further details needed for understanding the difference between knowing and not knowing?'

3.2 Building a theory of knowledge: belief?

Where should we begin? Here is the simplest theory of knowledge that someone might propose:

Knowing = Believing

This does not say merely that knowing involves believing. It *equates* knowing with believing. It says that any belief is knowledge – and vice versa.

Consider an example: 'I know that God exists and loves me. My faith is a form of belief. I need nothing more, for knowing of Him and His goodness. Fundamental religious *knowledge* is religious *belief*. And fundamental religious knowledge is the purest form of knowledge.' Yet does such a view accurately describe what it is to know that God exists? It conveys sincerity, a comforting feeling. But what if there is no God? Couldn't someone have that same strong feeling, experiencing that same inner sincerity, even if there is no God? The person would not be expressing or describing real knowledge; she would have *merely* a feeling of knowing that God exists. So, even if knowing includes believing, it is more than believing.

Remember, too, that some people believe, honestly and earnestly, that the Earth is flat. Must we allow, just because they are sincere, that they know of the Earth's being flat? And have you read George Orwell's famous 1949 book, *Nineteen Eighty-Four*, in which the hero, Winston Smith, comes – after torture and brainwashing – to believe that 2 + 2 = 5? He believes, he really does; yet he has not gained knowledge.

Take another example. Almost everyone both believes and knows that 2 + 2 = 4. But having the *belief* is not a full explanation of having the *knowledge*. Someone could have the belief because she learned '2 + 2 = 4' by rote, when she was a trusting infant. It was just a form of words for her. We do not understand her having the knowledge, simply by describing her as having the belief. Knowing is more complicated.

So, having a particular belief – no matter how convincing it feels – is not enough for having knowledge. There is more to knowing than believing. This is so, even when a belief is socially widespread. Not everything that is conventionally accepted must be knowledge. Groups disagree with other groups. Large groups can include disagreements within their ranks. Even when there is collective agreement, this could be due to a shared group delusion, say: if one person can believe from ignorance (even while feeling knowledgeable), so might a group of people. We must say more, if we are to understand how knowing differs from not knowing.

3.3 Building a theory of knowledge: true belief?

What was missing from that initial attempt to formulate a theory of knowledge (on which knowing is merely believing)? One answer is clear. *Truth* is needed within knowledge: it is not enough to feel correct in what one says or thinks; actually being correct is needed. Knowing is at least that kind of success. It includes being accurate, being right. It includes truth.

This gives us a slightly more complex conception of knowledge's nature:

> Knowing = Believing accurately
>   = Having a true belief, an accurate belief

When a belief fails to be knowledge, is this always due to falsity (mistake, inaccuracy)? Is truth (accuracy) all that is ever needed, if a belief is to be knowledge? This new conception implies so.

That remains a temptingly simple picture of knowing's nature. But is it too simple? Imagine being a jury member in a murder trial. Like your fellow jurors, you are swayed by the prosecuting lawyer's velvety words. These seem to be good evidence of guilt. Really, though, their evidence is flimsy. Does that matter? Those velvety words lead you to believe that the defendant is guilty. And, two years later, DNA evidence is found that ... confirms the defendant's guilt: your belief was accurate! Yet was it knowledge? Did you leave that jury room, knowing that the defendant had committed the crime? If not (as most would agree), this must be for a reason *other* than your belief's being false – since actually it was true. Your belief, although true, lacked some *further* needed feature; this is why it was not knowledge. (And does this matter? Section 6.3.1 will discuss knowing and the death penalty.)

What else is needed, then, in our picture of how knowing differs from not knowing?

3.4 Building a theory of knowledge: a third element?

The courtroom case suggests that *genuinely good evidence*, such as DNA evidence, is what makes a true belief knowledge. In some or another form, that suggestion has long been accepted by epistemologists. I will describe three of those forms (before synthesizing them, in section 3.5, into a unified theory of knowledge).

3.4.1 Logos

This element of epistemology began with Plato. From two of his dialogues (the *Meno* and the *Theaetetus*, mentioned in sections 1.6 and 2.2) came the idea that knowing includes having in mind a pertinent *logos*. This ancient Greek word is usually translated as 'account' or 'explanation'. So, the idea is that knowing includes having in mind an explanatory understanding of what is being known. More simply, knowing that something is true includes *understanding how* it is true.

As a juror in section 3.3's case, you believed that the defendant was guilty, and you were correct. Suppose that the evidence presented in court was only about the defendant's motivation, revealing nothing – no explanatory *understanding* – of the 'mechanics' of *how* the killing was performed. By the definition of '*logos*', this evidence is not a *logos* for the belief in the defendant's guilt. So, even when the DNA evidence arrives, you have no *logos* in mind supporting your belief: you have good evidence, but no *logos*. Hence, if we continue saying that you lack knowledge of the guilt, in spite of having the DNA evidence, we could be asking you to have in mind an appropriate *logos* before your belief can be knowledge. We could be saying that you need to understand *how* the belief is true.

3.4.2 *Good evidence*

Alternatively, suppose we say that the DNA evidence – in spite of not being a *logos* for you in this case – does make your true belief knowledge. Then we are not requiring you to have in mind a *logos* before your belief can be knowledge. But we can be requiring you to have in mind *good evidence* (such as the DNA evidence) – even if not always evidence amounting to a *logos*. After all, although a *logos* is a form of evidence, it is not the only possible kind of evidence: not all evidence is a *logos*, because not all evidence provides *explanatory* understanding. A *logos* is a particularly insightful form of evidence, of *how* the belief being supported by it is true. Mostly, even good evidence is not a *logos*.

This is because a *logos* has a special sort of content. Again, it is an account of *how* a belief is true: it is explanatory. But evidence in general is more like a *sign*: it is a sign that a belief is true, not necessarily an explanation of how the belief is true. Not everything telling us that something is true tells us how it is true. Most evidence is a more partial or fragmentary indication of truth than a *logos* is. Good evidence is usually more like a *single street sign*, a helpful but small indication of part of the overall direction in which we should be travelling. A *logos* is more like a *complete map* of the area through which we plan to travel, with our destination marked clearly on that map.

For example, good evidence is vital to good science. But, even in science, good evidence can help without being a *logos*: it can point us towards a truth without revealing nature's inner working underlying that truth. Think of a series of experiments used by a scientist to test an hypothesis. The experiments give her good evidence in support of the hypothesis – which, let us suppose, is true. We might therefore regard this hypothesis as scientific knowledge – a true (scientific) belief supported by good (scientific) evidence.

Or think of an historian, reading widely on a specific period and country. Ensconced in an ancient library, she consults source after source. On and on this could continue. But it does not. There comes a day when the historian decides that she has enough evidence, with one particular hypothesis now standing out from its competitors: her evidence points – not conclusively, but firmly – to its being true. Suppose that this favoured hypothesis *is* true. It seems that the researcher has gained historical knowledge – a true (historical) belief supported by good (historical) evidence.

But her evidence, like the scientist's, although a good sign of the truth of the hypothesis being tested, is not quite a *logos* for that hypothesis. Each body of evidence – the scientific evidence, the historical evidence – *points towards* one hypothesis, favouring it over competitors. In each case, the evidence includes data – scientific data, historical data – that are best explained by the favoured scientific/historical hypothesis. In neither case, though, need the evidence be *an account of how* the hypothesis is true.

3.4.3 Appropriate circumstances

We have seen that having a *logos* in mind is one way to have good evidence in mind. But does knowing always require 'good evidence in mind' at all (be the evidence a *logos* or not)? Instead, should we allow that knowing can sometimes be one's having a true belief *in appropriate circumstances*, quite apart from whether one's mind includes evidence of those circumstances?

Here are some examples of what this idea might encompass.

Suppose that you are a reliable source of information – reliable at producing true beliefs – on the whereabouts, at any time, of the US President. How do you accomplish this? By attending to news reports? No. You have an innate power of ESP, uncannily attuned always to the President's location! You do not know this about yourself. You have never noticed it. But this ESP capacity of yours works well – repeatedly, always unnoticed. Are these beliefs of yours knowledge (each time, of the President's location) due to your ESP in fact being so reliable about this? Does it matter that you never have in mind any accompanying evidence (let alone a *logos*) to support the truth of these beliefs 'gifted' to you by ESP?

Less fancifully, most of us have some accurate (true) beliefs that we hold confidently without any good evidence. I cannot recall all of the good evidence upon which I have ever relied; my mind is not powerful enough! Think for a moment. Bring to mind a *belief* for which, long ago, you had good evidence – a belief, however, for which you can no longer bring to mind that evidence. You might even be unable to remember where to find the evidence. (Often, I can recall a book in which to locate some evidence, even when I cannot remember the evidence itself. Sometimes, though, I cannot do even this.) Still, might that not matter? If you did have good evidence, or were reliably taught this material while young, is this enough? Can your current true belief be knowledge anyway, because you gained it in a way that was appropriate for knowing at the time, even if that 'way' is now only an historical circumstance, long forgotten by you? Can the belief be knowledge anyway for you?

3.5 Building a theory of knowledge: justified true belief

Have we done enough to describe the basic differences between knowing and not knowing?

First we identified knowing as involving these elements:

- having a belief
- the belief's being true (accurate)

But that, it seemed, is not enough: a belief can be true without being knowledge. What else is needed, if a true belief is to be knowledge? We considered these possibilities:

- having in mind a *logos* (the idea of this comes from Plato)

- having in mind good evidence (this is a generalization of the idea of a *logos*)
- being in appropriate circumstances, with these not needing to be present to one's mind.

We noted that epistemologists usually group these together, under one general idea. This general idea is standardly referred to with the word 'justification':

A belief is *justified* (in the sense we have been discussing) for someone if it is well supported by a *logos* in her mind, or more generally by *good evidence* in her mind, or if it is held by her in an *appropriate circumstance*.

Aha! With all of that in hand, we arrive at an important stage in our thinking. We have reached what philosophers call a *justified-true-belief* theory of knowledge:

One's having some specific knowledge = (1) one's having *enough justification in support* of a specific proposition + (2) the proposition's being *true* + (3) one's *believing* that the proposition is true.

    For short: knowledge = justification + truth + belief

    For shorter: knowledge = justified true belief. (For instance, one's knowing that one is a person = one's having a justified true belief that one is a person.)

    For shortest: K = JTB.

Notice how this theory is a philosophical *analysis* (philosophers often call it a 'conceptual analysis') of knowing's nature. It tries to understand knowing's presence analytically (in the sense described within section 3.1). It aims to 'break down' by analysing – thereby revealing – some of the complexity within knowing. The goal is to describe the key elements within any instance of knowledge. This will show how knowing differs from not knowing. First we find those 'inner' parts; then we show how they can be combined to produce an instance of knowing.

By the way, we need to be careful with the term 'justification'. There are at least three senses of justification (even when it is applied just to beliefs):

- *pragmatic* justification (= its being good, in a practical way, to have a specific belief);
- *moral* justification (= its being good, in a moral way, to have a specific belief);
- *epistemic* justification (= its being good, in a 'knowing way', to have a specific belief).

The last of those is our intended sense of justification – however, exactly, we should understand it.

Care is also needed with the term 'epistemic'. Section 1.6 mentioned that it comes from the ancient Greek word '*epistēmē*' (= 'knowledge'), as do the words 'epistemology' and 'epistemological'. I repeat this to emphasise the importance of not confusing the word 'epistemic' with the word 'epistemological'. To call X *epistemic* is to describe X as having to do with knowledge. To call Y *epistemological* is to describe Y as involving *theorising about* something's (such as X's) being epistemic. Epistemology is the philosophical study of whatever is epistemic. A belief's being knowledge is its having *the epistemic property* of being knowledge. Our thinking philosophically about that epistemic property is our *being epistemological* about it.

3.6 Theorizing about knowing's components

So the chapter's initial challenge has now been met. We have in hand a theory of knowledge. We have built the theory carefully, in a few steps (through the previous few sections). This has been an exercise in being episte-mological: we have sought – step by step by step – to describe the difference, in general terms, between knowing and not knowing. Of course, theories need to be tested and refined – which is what the next chapter will do with our theory. Before then, we can think further about the theory's components.

After all, ultimately our philosophical theory of knowledge should be part of our philosophical picture of ... everything! It should link instructively with other theories, including theories of those components within knowing that it says are part of knowing. We want theories that provide *independent* understanding of belief, of truth, and of epistemic justification. If we do not understand those three phenomena, we do not understand knowledge, at least not well, by saying that it is composed of them.

Here are a few comments, reflecting on those three components.

Belief. Are you always aware of all of your beliefs? Or are some of them hidden even from yourself? There was a time when all mental activity was assumed to be present to consciousness. That is no longer the usual view. Psychologists, it seems, often help with uncovering elusive beliefs. Even so, beliefs can remain unnoticed. Some might be revealed, though, in what you *do* (including what you say). Think, too, of mathematical beliefs: you have so so *so* many of these that you never bring to mind; yet in moving your body, you implicitly respect reality's mathematical nature; and you could easily give voice to many further mathematical beliefs. The follow-ing two possible features of belief are worth noting.

- A belief might be a potential, a disposition – even without being expressed in action, even without being noticed. Believing includes *hypothetical* actions (such as hypothetical comments or answers): *if* asked 'What is that animal?', you *would* reply, 'It's a kangaroo.'

The idea is that this potential – even if it remains only a potential – action is literally part of your believing (even if you are never actually asked that question, and hence never reply) that the animal is a kangaroo.

- A belief might be more, or less, strongly present (be it expressed or not). You can believe more, or less, strongly that the animal in front of you is a kangaroo, regardless of whether you ever express this belief in words. Perhaps there are degrees of belief, culminating only sometimes in a full belief (which would reflect a total commitment to its being true).

Truth. A belief's being true is essential to its being knowledge. No one can know a falsehood, since to know is to know as-true. One can know (the truth) that some proposition is false. But one cannot know (as true) the false proposition itself.

- We might distinguish between *truths* and *facts*. We could say that a truth is a true claim, belief, or proposition (these being *bearers* of truth) – and a fact is what *makes* a truth true. I am an Australian. That is a fact 'in the world': perhaps it is an arrangement of atoms and social realities. It *makes* true the claim, belief, or proposition that I am an Australian. My belief that I am an Australian is thereby a truth – a truth about a corresponding fact.
- We should not confuse a belief's being *true* with there being *evidence* (epistemic justification) supporting it. People often say, 'No, that cannot be true. There is evidence, perhaps good evidence, *against* its being true.' But that thinking is confused. Whether there is *evidence* for, or against, a belief's being true is one thing; whether the belief *is* true is another thing. Showing the falsity of someone's evidence for a claim does not show that the claim is false.
- Truth might take different forms for different topics. For instance, are beliefs expressing moral truths made

true by moral facts? Or are there no moral facts? Could this be so, even if there are facts about the physical world that make true some beliefs expressing physical-world truths?

Epistemic justification. We have seen in a general way how knowledge's justification component might take different shapes. Further details will emerge in the next chapter. But one point should be made clear now: justification within knowledge needs to be *actually* good, not just apparently good. At times, we are *mistaken* about whether some particular evidence provides good support for a specific view. Even if it seems or feels like it does, that appearance or feeling could be misleading. How do we overcome this danger? Usually, we seek *more* evidence. This is not guaranteed to resolve the issue conclusively. What else can we do, though, when trying to decide rationally what is really justified and really true?

3.7 Knowledge as understanding?

We have taken a potentially significant step towards having in mind a useful picture of knowledge's nature. That picture, if accurate, amounts to some *understanding* of knowledge's nature. But what if understanding is itself a kind of *knowledge*? In doing epistemology (and hence seeking understanding of what knowledge is), are we actually seeking a kind of knowledge of what knowledge is?

That depends. Knowledge and understanding are at least not *worlds* apart in their natures. Imagine knowing everything about the world: your beliefs would recognize or record every truth that there is. Then presumably you would also understand the world completely – in all of its detailed splendour.

But that is an unlikely outcome. And when we make the example more realistic, so that you know only part of all that there is (by knowing just some of the world's facts), it no longer follows that you understand the world in those respects. It will depend on *what* your knowing includes, particularly in its justification component. We have considered three general forms that justification can take within knowledge:

1 *Logos* (section 3.4.1). Suppose that your knowing that you are seeing a sheep, for instance, includes your having in mind a *logos* – an account, some explanatory principles – underlying what a sheep is and what sight is. Then seemingly your knowledge *is* an understanding of the world in this respect (namely, the fact of your seeing a sheep).

2 *Good evidence* (section 3.4.2). Suppose that your knowing that you are seeing a sheep is based on normal sensory evidence ('That looks like a sheep'), and on normal evidence of how to use the words 'seeing' and 'sheep'. But suppose that you do not have in mind a *logos* (account, principles) about the nature of seeing or the nature of sheep. Then it seems that you have some knowledge *without* understanding: you know a fact (of your seeing a sheep) without understanding that fact's 'inner working'. Your evidence is like a *sign* to you of your seeing a sheep – without revealing or explaining to you the 'inner what-it-is' of your seeing a sheep.

3 *Appropriate circumstances* (section 3.4.3). If having good evidence in mind is like being aware of a sign, then simply *being in* appropriate circumstances is like being *unconsciously guided by* a sign. Suppose that you glance distractedly yet reliably at the field, only unconsciously registering the sheep's presence. Perhaps you do still know (unconsciously, in a dispositional way) that you see a sheep. But it does

not seem that you are *understanding* – delving in an explanatory way into – the fact of your seeing a sheep. (This is not to say that you are *mis*understanding that fact. Maybe you are knowing it just in a more 'superficial' way. Sections 5.13.3 and 5.13.4 will say more about this idea.)

3.8 Knowledge's value

We have been investigating the difference between knowing and not knowing. But why does this matter? Is there any distinctive *value* in knowing (as against not knowing)? This takes us to the heart of the value in epistemology itself: *it* matters, if knowing matters. Epistemology might matter differently to how the knowing matters; still, it matters *somehow* if knowing matters. Here is a relevant analogy: particle physics matters, if fundamental particles matter. Particle physics might matter differently to how the particles matter; still, it matters *somehow* if those particles matter.

So, *do* fundamental particles matter? Presumably, their doing so would reflect their role within whatever *happens* in reality. Without those particles, maybe little or nothing happens. In a similar vein, we might wonder about knowledge. Can it have indirect – *instrumental* – value? Can knowing have a value that amounts to its functioning as an instrument – a tool, a means to an end – that might help us? Without knowledge, maybe little or nothing *happens* that is humanly important. Can knowledge be valuable because of how it helps us to act – to *do* things – with it, or as a result of having it?

That question has an ancient lineage. We noted (in section 3.4.1) Plato's advocating, in the *Meno*, that knowledge is a true belief (opinion) accompanied by a *logos*. He motivated this idea by describing how it allowed knowledge to contribute to an *action* that Socrates and Meno were discussing – namely, journeying to Larissa. Socrates allowed that having a *true belief* about how to reach Larissa would – if held firmly in mind – be as effective in that respect as *knowledge* of how to reach Larissa would be. But Socrates argued that a true belief that falls short of being knowledge is unlikely to be held firmly in mind.

This argument from Socrates is famous among philosophers. He claimed that a true belief without a *logos* – a true belief falling short of knowledge – would be like one of Daedalus' legendary statues. Why were these legendary? Simple: they had the capacity to move! Yes, indeed: if not tethered in place, they would run away. And this, contended Socrates, is what true beliefs do when no *logos* accompanies them: even a true belief about how to reach Larissa will not stay, guiding one to journey's end, if one does not hold in mind an accompanying *logos*. In contrast (claimed Socrates), knowledge does include a *logos*: it is a *tethered* true belief – like Daedalus' remarkable statues, once tethered in place. (Think here of the difference between remembering a correct exam answer, and – more reassuringly – remembering it while also knowing how to recreate it if need be, courtesy of understanding it.) Knowledge is thus deemed to be especially powerful and useful – because of the *logos* within it. This *logos* keeps the knowledge in place, by keeping the true belief in place. The knowledge remains present to one's mind, enabled to continue guiding one's actions. Knowing is thereby notably valuable, because it is so good at guiding us through life.

Our final chapter will revisit that potentially reassuring claim, by developing some *applied* epistemology – discussing practical ways in which knowledge, and thinking about knowledge, might assist us. (A hint of what is to come: we will be discussing love, life, racism, God, abortion, history and much more.) Before then, as I indicated, we should refine, and test more thoroughly, this chapter's theory of knowledge. The aim is to formulate it as well as we can, *before* using it to understand how knowing, for example, functions within humanly and socially pressing kinds of situation. We need to be justifiedly confident of *what* knowledge is, before we can be justifiedly confident about why knowing can matter – how it can have value – in those worldly ways.

4

Refining Our Theory
of Knowledge

4.1 Our theory thus far

The story thus far ... we now have in hand a theory of knowledge, ready to be used. It is a short theory, saying simply that knowledge is a well justified true belief: a belief is only ever knowledge by being accurate (true) and well justified (such as by good evidence).

Take an example. How does our theory analyse your knowing that the animal swimming in front of you is a dolphin? Here is how. You have a belief ('That's a dolphin'). It is true (the animal really is a dolphin). And you have good evidence supporting it (your eyesight is good, you have read informative books about dolphins).

That is what knowing looks like, if our theory is correct. What about *not* knowing? According to the theory, to lack some specific knowledge is to *fail* one or more of the theory's three conditions for knowing. (This might happen without one's noticing it: a person can *mistakenly* think that she has some specific knowledge.) For example,

- you would not *believe* that the animal is a dolphin (maybe you lose confidence in visually identifying dolphins); and/or
- you would not *actually* be looking at a dolphin (it might be a porpoise); and/or
- you would lack *good enough* evidence of the animal's being a dolphin (perhaps you lack access to any good scientific sources that differentiate precisely between dolphins and porpoises).

So, we have this picture:

> Knowing = satisfying three conditions at once (truth, belief, and good justification).
>
> Not knowing = failing one or more of those three conditions (lacking truth and/or belief and/or good justification).

Should that theory be accepted, given the care that we have taken in formulating it?

Well, it *is* an excellent theory. It possesses some notable virtues, ones that we generally want theories to have.

1 It is a *simple* theory. Other things being equal, simpler theories are preferable to more complex ones.
2 It seems to be *internally coherent*. It apparently combines elements – talking of truth, belief, and justification – that fit together in natural ways.
3 It seems to link well with *further* philosophical theories – such as theories of truth, of belief, and of justification. It therefore promises to fit into a *larger* philosophical picture of ourselves and the world.

All of this speaks in favour of adopting the justified-true-belief theory of knowledge: it seems to be a *good* theory. Still, even this does not prove that the theory is true. How should we decide whether to accept it?

Here is an answer that might initially sound puzzling: we could *attack* the theory. We would be *testing* the theory. Any theory needs to be strong in practice. It needs to accommodate, explain, and predict suitable data. Will we find data that our theory of knowledge *cannot* explain – data conflicting dramatically with the theory? Indeed, can we find unshakeable data like that – data *showing* the theory to be false? If we can, we should discard the theory. If we cannot, we should retain the theory – at least for now.

4.2 The Stopped Clock

Here is a first important datum.

In 1948, Bertrand Russell described a possible situation that has since struck many people as showing the falsity of the justified-true-belief theory of knowledge. I say 'since', because Russell directed his case only against the simpler theory of knowledge-as-true-belief (section 3.3). Here is a fuller version of his story, a version directed at the justified-true-belief theory of knowledge:

> A person, walking along, sees a clock. She notes the time: 'It's 11:23. I must hurry.' She speeds onwards, reacting to what was actually the correct time being displayed by the clock. But it was a stopped clock! Precisely twenty-four hours earlier, it had stopped at ... yes, 11:23. So, the person's belief – 'It's 11:23' – was *true* (accurate). She also had *good evidence* for her belief's being true: as she instantaneously realized (without reminding herself of it), clocks generally work reliably, as do her eyes. Hence, at that moment she had a *well justified true belief* (that the time is 11:23). Yet did she have *knowledge* (of the time's being 11:23)? Few, if any, people will concede so.

Russell was not reporting an actual event, as far as I know. But that is irrelevant, because it is a realistically possible case, one that could easily occur. Our data can be actual cases *or* possible ones, because we want our theory to be that powerful, telling us about all actual *and* all possible knowledge. So, we need to understand the implications even of a case like Russell's. *Why* is the belief in question ('It's 11:23') not knowledge?

The answer might seem clear: the clock's being stopped, and thus its not working properly, prevents the belief from being knowledge. Yet is this all that matters? What of the person's *not realizing* that the clock is stopped? Already, then, we have two possible details to consider: the clock is stopped, and the person does not notice this.

But how should we use those details? Can we turn them into an understanding *more generally* of how knowing differs from not knowing? We will discuss some diagnostic options in section 4.5. First, though, what does this case actually establish? It seems to show that our theory ('knowledge = justified true belief') is not really understanding *all possible* situations where knowledge is at stake. After all, this possible situation includes a justified true belief that *fails* to be knowledge. Hence, our theory, as currently formulated, cannot be quite right, given its clashing with this specific case.

Seemingly, therefore, our theory needs to say more about what knowing is. What should that 'more' be? How should we amend our theory? We could aim for an instance of 'knowledge = justified true belief *plus* ... .' Plus *what*, though? Plus further details *within* one of those three elements (justification, truth, belief)? Or plus a wholly new *kind* of element, in addition to those three?

4.3 Gettier cases

Perhaps we need further data, beyond a single imagined case. Would having further data help us to generalize more widely and wisely, to an adequate theory covering all possible situations where knowing is at stake?

In 1963, epistemologists began gathering much data. In 1963, this issue strode forcefully to the front-and-centre of epistemology's world-stage, glaring at the audience. This happened with the publication of a brief article by an American philosopher Edmund Gettier.

Gettier told two imagined stories. Each was more complex than Russell's. Each was presented as showing that a belief's being true and justified is not enough to guarantee its being knowledge. Gettier's article generated an enormous amount of philosophical discussion; it continues doing so. Almost all epistemologists, then and since, have regarded Gettier's argument as a datum that decisively disproves the justified-true-belief theory of knowledge. This spurred many of those epistemologists to respond constructively, by reflecting on Gettier's article in order to *rebuild* their suddenly crumbling – the discredited-by-Gettier – theory of knowledge.

That rebuilding soon had an abundance of data with which to work. There were Gettier's two cases, along with many more, akin to his two, that appeared in epistemological writings. Here is one of the simpler cases (adapted from American philosopher Roderick Chisholm's 1966 version):

Standing outside a field, seeing what looks like a sheep, someone thinks, 'There is a sheep in that field.' Her belief is true (accurate): unseen by her (it is behind a hill), there *is* a sheep in that field. The person is seeing only a disguised dog – a dog in sheep's clothing! Even so, the person is using what feels to her like normal perceptual evidence: the light is good, her eyesight is good, the animal seems to be a normal sheep. Thus, the person has a *belief* (that there is a sheep in the field) *that is true and well justified*. Yet is it *knowledge* (that there is a sheep in the field)? Surely not.

Why would that justified true belief not be knowledge? Epistemologists seek a general answer, a theoretical understanding of all knowledge, even when reacting to a particular case like this. What do we learn from this specific case, along with similar ones, about knowledge in general?

That phrase 'similar ones' is important. It directs us to what soon entered epistemology as a new interpretive category (along with a new term). The idea of *a Gettier case* encompassed Gettier's original two stories, plus the multitude of similar ones (such as the sheep-in-the-field case) that appeared in books and academic journal articles. Different Gettier cases differ in details. But a generic characterization has persisted: each Gettier case includes *a justified true belief that – according to most epistemologists – fails to be knowledge.*

Accordingly, the textbook view of the inadequacy revealed by Gettier cases is this: the justified-true-belief theory *insufficiently* describes how to distinguish, in a theoretical and understanding way, between knowing and not knowing. Gettier cases show that a belief could satisfy what the justified-true-belief theory says is enough for being knowledge, even *without* the belief's being knowledge. Hence, the theory does not say enough about what makes something an instance of knowing. Something extra must be mentioned if we are to understand what knowing is.

4.4 The fake barns

We should be aware of another puzzling case. Most epistemologists view it as a Gettier case. First published in 1976 by an American philosopher Alvin Goldman, it is generally called 'the fake-barns case'. Here is a version of how it begins:

> Henry is driving in the countryside with his young son. Early on, Henry points out of the window, saying 'That's

a barn.' Because it is indeed a barn, he has a *true* belief ('That's a barn'). And his belief is *justified*, since Henry sees the barn in a normal way, using good eyesight in good light, not driving too quickly. Is his justified true belief knowledge?

So far, that description of the situation gives us no reason to deny that the belief is knowledge. But wait: the story continues.

Without realizing it, Henry is in an unusual neighbourhood, containing many *fake* barns. Viewed from the road, these facsimiles – this is what they are! – look like real barns. If one of these had been attracting Henry's attention, he would again have believed 'That's a barn.' Yet he would have been mistaken, fooled by a facsimile.

There is a sense, we might say, in which Henry is *lucky* to have formed his true belief, working with the sort of evidence that he has. Because of those fake barns, he could easily have had *misleading* evidence (of his seeing a barn, when he would have been looking at a fake) that would have seemed the same to him as his actually accurate evidence does. In that alternative possible situation, he would have been fooled without noticing it. Hence, we might feel that his actually not being fooled has been due largely to luck. And so he is actually not gaining knowledge. Although he gains a perceptually *justified true belief*, it is not perceptual *knowledge* (of the object's being a barn).

4.5 Possible refinements

We have met the stopped clock, the dog in sheep's clothing, and the fake barns. We now have the concept of a Gettier case. Armed with all that new data, it is time to confront the challenge of revising our justified-true-belief theory of knowledge. Maybe the theory will require lots of tinkering; maybe only a little. Remember (from section 3.1) that our aim is to formulate a theory saying only what *needs* to be said – not wasting words – as we build it, step by step. But now – thanks to Russell and Gettier – it seems that a further step of theory-building could be needed, taking us *beyond* our justified-true-belief theory.

How might we approach this? We can regard Gettier cases as illustrating *wrong* ways to be justified (even though within each Gettier case a true belief is reached), when knowledge is at stake. Perhaps describing a true belief simply as *justified* (as the justified-true-belief theory does) is too generic – not sufficiently detailed and precise – for distinguishing between knowing and not knowing. What might – if we are to speak in more detail – be *right* ways to be justified, when knowledge is at stake? Since 1963, epistemologists have offered many suggestions. I will mention a few.

4.5.1 Eliminating significant false evidence

Chapter 3 talked in a general way of *good* evidence as possibly being needed within knowing. Does thinking about Gettier cases help us to be more specific than that?

In the sheep-in-the-field case, for instance, might the problem be that the person's belief ('There is a sheep in that field') is based on some *false* evidence? (The evidence is her response to the animal that she is seeing. She does not realize that it is a disguised dog, a dog dressed in a sheep's fleece.) Should we refine our theory in the following way?

> Knowing = Having a true belief that is well justi-
> fied – without relying on any false evidence.

That revision would apparently give the correct verdict on the sheep-in-the-field case (by implying that the belief is not knowledge, due to some false evidence being used). So far, so good. But we need to go further in our thinking. We want a *general* picture of what knowledge is, doing justice to *all* possible situations where knowledge is present, along with *all* of those where it is not. And does the suggested refinement mistakenly classify, as not being knowledge, some beliefs that are knowledge? Consider a complicated scientific research project involving a lot of evidence, some of which is false. If enough true (accurate) evidence is used, maybe a small amount of false evidence is acceptable. Perhaps scientific knowledge is being produced, even if some false evidence is involved.

Should we therefore apply a qualitative standard, not a quantitative one, to how false evidence affects knowing? We might say that justification's being good enough to be providing knowledge is less about the *number* of falsehoods within one's evidence, and more about the evidence's not relying on *significant* falsehoods:

> Knowing = Having a true belief that is well justified – without relying on any significantly false evidence.

That is easy to say, less easy to apply. *When* is a falsehood within evidence for a belief's truth so significant as to prevent the belief's being knowledge? Perhaps no single answer applies to every possible instance of knowledge. Even so, we might adopt this practical moral:

> When knowing is at stake, one needs to check more diligently than usual for whether one's evidence includes any falsity that should be worrying.

4.5.2 Not overlooking significant truths

We have noted that evidence can include falsity without this chasing away knowledge. What about when evidence has gaps – by not mentioning every related truth?

Again we might adopt a qualitative approach: perhaps some gaps in evidence are significant, while some are not. Gettier cases seem to involve evidence with significant gaps. In these, the evidence fails to include a truth that, apparently, *needs* to have been included, if knowledge was to be gained. When a fact is overlooked, and this weakens the quality of the evidence so much that the belief based on the evidence is not knowledge, that fact is called a 'defeater': we might call it a *significant defeater*. A significant gap in one's evidence – a gap that chases away the knowledge in question – is one's overlooking a significant defeater.

For example, with the sheep-in-the-field case, we might say that the observed animal's actually being a dog is a significant defeater. If the person outside the field had not overlooked this fact about the observed animal (its being a disguised dog), presumably she would not have formed her belief ('There is a sheep in that field') in the first place – because then her evidence would *not* have encouraged her to have that belief.

Should our theory of knowledge therefore be changed to something like this (which is typically called a *defeasibility* account of knowledge's nature)?

> Knowing = Having a true belief that is well justified – with no significant defeater being overlooked by one's evidence.

And what about combining that proposed amendment with the previous one (in section 4.5.1)? We would then be requiring evidence, when knowledge is at stake, to be good at avoiding falsity *and* at including truth:

> Knowing = Having a true belief that is well justi-
> fied – without the evidence either including some-
> thing significantly false or overlooking a significant
> defeater.

The idea is that evidence good enough to be part of
knowing balances two important needs: it takes into
account *actually* significant truths, and it is not mistaken in what it *treats* as significant truths.

It is difficult in practice to know whether one's evidence includes falsity. It is also difficult to know that
one is not overlooking a significant defeater. After all,
if one's evidence overlooks a significant defeater, how
is one simultaneously to be aware of it? Still, one can
be vigilant, staying alert to whether one has *been* overlooking significant defeaters. One can be awake to the
potential need to *revise* whatever one has been thinking.
One can thus remain active as a thinker, open to the
possibility of changing one's mind in response to better
evidence, if knowledge is to be the result.

4.5.3 Eliminating luck

People often comment on the *luck* that seems to operate
within Gettier cases. What would this involve? Suppose
that you satisfy the revised theory from a moment ago:
your evidence has the right balance of inclusion and
exclusion. It includes no significant falsity. It overlooks
no significant facts (more specifically, no significant
defeaters). This balance lessens any *need* for luck if you
are to use your evidence to form a true belief. Without
that balance, it is more likely that you could form a true
belief *only* through luck when relying on your (unbal-
anced) evidence.

In the sheep-in-the-field case, remember, the person is misled by looking at what is not really a sheep. So, her perceptual evidence's nonetheless producing a true belief relies significantly on luck – counteracting what the falsity in her evidence made much more likely.

Now consider the fake-barns case. If Henry had been aware of the area's containing many fake barns, he would not have formed the same belief ('That's a barn'). As it happens, he did form that belief, and it is true. But this combination (this belief plus its being true) was unlikely, *given* the area's including those fake barns, a significant fact overlooked by his evidence. Henry has been lucky to form his true belief, given what his evidence overlooks.

Should we therefore refine our theory further, in the following way?

Knowing = Having a true belief that is well justified – without significant luck being involved in that justification's leading to that true belief.

We might explain this lack of significant luck via the alteration suggested in section 4.5.2: the evidence includes no significant falsity and overlooks no significant defeater. Are we continuing to improve our description of what distinguishes knowing from not knowing?

4.5.4 Being intellectually virtuous

Sections 4.5.1 and 4.5.2 talked of being careful, of trying not to rely on significantly false evidence, and trying not to overlook significant facts, if one is to gain knowledge. Then (in section 4.5.3) we saw how that picture's appeal could increase if we view it as describing a way of not needing significant luck to be gaining one's true belief from one's justification.

We might add a further idea to that mixture. If one is to avoid needing significant luck in reaching a true belief from one's justification, then one might need evidence with an appropriate blend of falsity-avoidance and truth-inclusion. But an important question arises even if one's evidence does satisfy that good blended standard. How is the evidence being *used*? Even having evidence with a nice blend of falsity-avoidance and truth-inclusion might not be enough to eliminate significant luck in one's reaching a true belief on the basis of that evidence. The evidence needs to be used *properly*, hence not too luckily.

For example, suppose that you have evidence with an excellent blend of falsity-avoidance and truth-inclusion, evidence supporting the proposition that you are looking at a dolphin. You then form the *belief* that you are looking at a dolphin. But suppose that you do this because (even while aware of your good evidence) you strongly *want* the animal to be a dolphin. (People can form beliefs for stranger reasons than that!) Then we have this result: although you have good evidence, you are not using it properly – as it should be used if it is to justify your belief so as to make the belief knowledge. Your motivation in forming the belief has been wishful thinking, not truth-seeking. So, it seems, another requirement on knowledge's being present is that the belief has been produced via a proper *motivation*.

But what makes one's motivation 'proper' when forming a belief on the basis of evidence? One popular view is that the evidence must be used in *intellectually virtuous* ways. (We might add that it is bespeaking no intellectual *vices*.) For instance, one should use one's evidence in an intellectually *responsible* way. Some people are motivated not only to find good evidence, but to use it carefully. Some people genuinely want to find truth, wherever it might be, rather than wanting mainly a belief that offers a satisfying social standing (such as a belief helping one to 'fit in' with a fancied set of people). Some people remain open, as a matter of character, to new evidence, including evidence telling them that they were previously mistaken.

But that is still not enough. Not *only* our motivations are important when forming beliefs that we hope are knowledge. Good intellectual *habits*, accompanying those motivations, are also vital. One's being a genuinely responsible inquirer is not simply one's wanting and intending to be like that. One needs to be motivated *and* effective. We might talk of a person's intellectual *character*. This is analogous to talking of her moral character. One could perform an action with a morally good *consequence*. (This would be like forming a belief that is *true*.) One could perform that action while being aware of a good reason why one should do it. (This would be like having good evidence supporting one's forming a true belief.) Yet what if one performs the action on a whim, even while aware of that good reason for doing it? In that case, one is not really caring about the consequence's being morally good. Would this lessen the action's moral goodness? We might regard this as analogous to one way for a justified true belief to fail to be knowledge: the justification needs not only to be present; it needs to be *used in an aptly virtuous way*, such as by reflecting one's caring about reaching truth.

Should we see knowing, then, as an achievement that comes only to those who deserve it – perhaps not morally, but *as inquirers*? Is knowing a reflection partly of cognitive or intellectual character? Simply being a person, even one who is capable of thinking well, is not enough, it might be said, for having an estimable intellectual character in action whenever one is thinking. Does knowing only ever come from acting in a way that genuinely reflects an intellectually good character?

Incidentally, there are many intellectual virtues; I have mentioned only a few. Being open-minded about new evidence and alternative viewpoints; being able to discard discredited evidence; sincerely caring about truth as such; being energetic in pursuing truth; being a reliable thinker, not a slovenly one; etc. This is potentially a fascinating list. Any longer version of it will reveal much about our potential for gaining knowledge. (Do not forget the possibility, too, of there being intellectual vices. This is similarly intriguing.)

For example, revisit the sheep-in-the-field case. Does the person within that case lack knowledge because her true belief (that there is a sheep in the field) is not reflecting, closely enough, her having and applying intellectual virtues? If it had been more closely tied to her intellectual virtues, she would not have *needed* so much luck – with the world luckily cooperating, counteracting what would otherwise have been her forming a false belief – in order to form her true belief ('There is a sheep in that field').

The account being suggested right now is what a *virtue* epistemologist might say. The resulting theory of knowledge could look like this:

Knowing = Having a true belief that is well justified – with the true belief arising as a reflection of the justification's being used in an intellectually virtuous way.

This can also be combined with our earlier ideas. Knowing would then be a matter of using evidence virtuously, while also not relying on significant falsity and not overlooking significant truths (and thereby not reaching a true belief too luckily).

4.6 Post-Gettier theorizing about knowledge

Where does all that back-and-forth analysing and theorizing leave us? We now have a *refined* justified-true-belief theory – one that has been refined a few times. It is not being advanced as definitely true. It is offered as possibly true, with much philosophical thought being devoted to these issues since 1963.

This has been a striking era within contemporary philosophy. By guiding us through those possible refinements, section 4.5 gives us a taste of *post-Gettier* epistemology. Responses to Gettier's challenge have sprouted. Some have blossomed. Some have withered. Some remain, still growing. Theories have been offered; counter-examples and concerns have arisen; revisions have occurred. All of this continues to happen. Throughout, the philosophical consensus has been that if we are to understand knowledge, we must understand what goes wrong within Gettier cases – *why* there is a lack of knowledge within them. Otherwise, we will not understand sufficiently the difference between knowing and not knowing. We will face an enormous hurdle in trying to make epistemological progress.

Of course, not all post-1963 epistemology has been post-Gettier epistemology, in the sense of according Gettier cases pride of place when theorizing about knowledge. The next section describes a growing strand within contemporary epistemology that does not always share the usual acceptance of Gettier cases as being so vital. Before then, though, what *is* that 'usual acceptance' by epistemologists, regarding Gettier cases? It has three main parts.

First, most epistemologists accept that, *whenever a belief is Gettiered* (that is, whenever a belief is at the heart of a Gettier case), *it fails to be knowledge.*

Second, most epistemologists infer from this that the initial (unrevised) justified-true-belief theory is false, needing somehow to be revised.

That is why section 4.5 guided us through some prominent post-Gettier thinking. Third, though, epistemologists are yet to *agree* on how to revise the justified-true-belief theory, in light of Gettier cases.

Can nothing useful be said, then, about what knowledge is? That might be needlessly defeatist. Suppose that we amend our theory in this minimal way:

> Knowing = Having a true belief that is well justified – but not in a way that is too similar to what happens within some Gettier case.

In practice, that might be helpful. Gettier cases arise in reality, but only rarely. So, for practical purposes, we could continue to treat knowing as having a well justified true belief. Seemingly, any mistakes that might occur when we do this will be few and far between. Epistemologists are confident in their ability to agree on whether a situation – once they know enough of its details – is a Gettier case. In practice, therefore, epistemologists easily agree that some justified true belief, once they espy its being inside a Gettier case, is not knowledge. This can happen even if epistemologists fail to agree on any fuller explanation of *why* the belief is not knowledge.

4.7 Experimental epistemology

Why have epistemologists been so confident about recognizing situations as Gettier cases? Why are they so confident that, when a belief is inside a Gettier case, it is not knowledge? *How* do we know that the person in the sheep-in-the-field case fails to know that there is a sheep in the field? *How* do we know that Henry fails to know that he is seeing a barn?

Epistemologists usually claim (in the spirit described in section 2.3.7) to be 'consulting their intuitions', or that it is 'intuitively obvious' what to say about such cases. Read or listen to an account of a Gettier case; reflect on it, while staying receptive to your inner voice, your power of intuition; supposedly, you will find yourself saying that those (Gettiered) beliefs are not knowledge. Nothing more is needed (we are told). This is a simple methodology, effortlessly available to everyone!

According to most epistemologists, those intuitive verdicts arrive clearly and easily when one reads or hears details of a Gettier case. Hence (it is often said), those intuitive verdicts are important *data* for our theorizing. As data about knowledge's nature, they should be shaping our theory of knowledge, so that it accommodates them. The intuitions reflect our shared view of *where* knowing differs from not knowing ('His belief is knowledge. Her belief is not knowledge'). We must refine our theory of knowledge to understand that difference. We can then say *how* knowing differs from not knowing, in light of Gettier cases. This might not be easy. It is made simpler, though, by our having such *firm* intuitive data about such cases.

But that comforting picture was questioned forcefully in 2001; and has continued being questioned. In that year, the initial article appeared in an academic philosophy journal on what was soon called *experimental* philosophy ('X-phi', for short). A major component of that article was some experimental *epistemology*. Apparently tired of philosophers agreeing merely with each other (and sometimes their students) as to what is 'intuitive', before using those 'intuitive' assessments to frame and test philosophical theories, three American philosophers (Jonathan Weinberg, Shaun Nichols, and Stephen Stich) took philosophy 'to the streets': they asked people *outside* academia for reactions to various philosophical stories. This included polling 'normal' people for reactions – *their* 'intuitive' reactions? – to some Gettier cases. A potentially new way of doing philosophy was unleashed upon the world! If we are to give such respect to intuitions, then (according to X-phi) we should at least be consulting a far wider range of people, to gain a better sense of what 'we' think about philosophy's test cases.

X-phi has become increasingly popular. Many philosophers are conducting such surveys, sometimes online, sometimes 'in the street'. For example, people could be given a description of the sheep-in-the-field case, before being asked whether they think that the belief in question ('There is a sheep in that field') fails to be knowledge.

Of course, this need not have resulted in anything surprising: however it is that philosophers react to such stories *might* have been exactly how other people do so. But in fact there was a surprising outcome. What surprised philosophers in 2001, and continues to exercise many philosophers' minds, is that a significant number of people being surveyed do *not* agree with philosophers' shared interpretation of Gettier cases, for instance. What is also interesting was that the initial surveys provided some evidence that not all racial, and not all socioeconomic, groupings shared those 'intuitive' views standardly championed by epistemologists – who are mainly male, of European ancestry, and not from a low socioeconomic band of society. In short, those reactions that were so easily shared by epistemologists (such as when responding to Gettier cases) were perhaps *not* so accurately representative of people in general. In which case, epistemologists' 'merely intuitive' reactions might *not* be hard-and-fast data, and might not *need* to be accommodated strictly by our finished theory of knowledge.

X-phi even opens the door to the potentially confronting possibility that, as epistemologists, we are not *obliged* to concede that each Gettiered belief (such as 'There is a sheep in that field' or 'That is a barn') fails to be knowledge. If enough non-philosophers (when asked, under properly controlled survey conditions) do not react as philosophers have done to Gettier cases, does this throw into disarray the history since 1963 of

post-Gettier epistemology? After all, post-Gettier epistemology has been built around the 'intuitive' view that
each Gettier case *does* contain a justified true belief
failing to be knowledge.

That potentially confronting possibility is starting to
be debated – a little. X-phi is a new way of raising it.
The philosophical jury is in the early stage of deliberating on what X-phi's lasting impact, if any, will be.

4.8 Understanding knowledge without analysing it?

Section 3.1 mentioned two general approaches to trying
to understand a phenomenon X. We have been following the first of those paths. Now is a good time to recall
the second one.

It asked whether we could understand X *without*
analysing X into component 'parts'. For example, can
we understand knowledge (a possible 'X') by *locating
it within a larger network* of phenomena? Could we
distinguish knowing from not knowing – so that we
understand knowledge's nature, *how* it is not not-know-
ing – by focusing on knowing's distinctive *roles* rather
than its inner components? Does understanding arise by
describing significant ways in which knowledge is *used*,
in which it therefore *matters*?

Here are two potentially significant roles that knowing
might play (described in general terms).

1 Does having appropriate knowledge *underlie
   successful actions*, allowing them to be actions at all?
   When moving your body as you wanted to move it,
   is this due partly to your knowledge – such as
   knowledge of an aim that you have, and knowledge
   of how people in general would act to satisfy that
   aim? For example, when an athlete moves well, must
   this reflect such knowledge?

2 Is knowledge conveyed *and transmitted in successful
   education*? Is knowledge a 'currency' of education?
   Is it part of the *point* of education?

One approach to trying to understand knowledge,
in these and other ways, without analysing its 'inner'
nature, has been called 'knowledge-first' epistemology.
The philosophical jury is also deliberating on what this
approach's lasting epistemological impact, if any, will
be. In any event, philosophical questions about the
practical nature and import of knowing can be independently important, as this book's final chapter will
demonstrate.

But before we get there, we will ask whether people
do actually have knowledge.

5

Is It Even Possible to Have Knowledge?

5.1 The basic idea of a sceptical argument

We have been constructing, testing, and refining a theory of knowledge. We have done this without deciding whether people *do* have knowledge. Strictly, we have been thinking more abstractly and hypothetically: what is it to know something, *if* knowing occurs?

So, let us now ask whether people actually do gain knowledge. Within epistemology, this question has long alluded to some eye-catching *sceptical* arguments. These develop – and then build dramatically upon – doubts about knowledge's even being possible for us. Sceptical arguments claim to uncover fundamental and inescapable limits upon our cognitive and intellectual capacities. (And why does this matter? Sceptical arguments can matter if we think of our lives as needing to be shaped *by* our having knowledge that matters. Section 3.8 discussed this potential value in knowing; in section 6.5 we will discuss it further.)

I used the terms 'possible', 'fundamental', and 'inescapable' just now. Sceptical challenges do not push you simply to 'think harder and smarter'. They say, more radically: 'No matter how hard you think, no matter how smart you are, you fail to gain knowledge.' Do not take this personally; everyone is being damned in this way! No human athlete can run 100 metres in a single second. It is physically impossible. Training harder cannot overcome this limitation. Sceptical arguments aim to highlight something similar: they claim that, no matter how hard we could ever try to know something, we fail.

5.2 The dreaming argument

Most sceptical arguments are not about *all* possible knowledge. Most focus on some specific kind of knowledge. Chapter 2 outlined different forms that knowing might take. Some of those forms have had famous sceptical arguments thrown at them. Probably the most famous of these arguments is *external world* scepticism. It doubts our ever having *observational* knowledge. One version of the argument goes like this:

Observational knowledge could arise only through perception. Imagine feeling that you are using your senses in a normal way. Perhaps surprisingly, even that feeling could be badly mistaken. You might be *dreaming*, without noticing it.

And how could you know that you are *not* dreaming? You cannot. Any attempt by you to check on whether you are dreaming might itself be part of your dreaming.

Hence, you are trapped. You can never know that you are not dreaming, even when feeling like you are sensing normally.

So, you can never have observational knowledge.

That is *the dreaming argument*. Its conclusion (when generalized, from you to everyone) is an *external world scepticism*. The term 'external world' refers to the physical world – which is 'external', in contrast to an 'inner' world of conscious experience. Even an experience that feels like a sensory interaction with the physical world ('I'm touching a tree, right here') need not really be so.

5.3 Sceptical reasoning, more generally

That formulation of external world scepticism is inspired by French philosopher René Descartes's classic version, in his 1641 'Meditation I'. So, it is often called *Cartesian* scepticism. Let us abstract from it, to a more *general* way of reasoning sceptically about knowledge. (Subsequent sections provide further instances of this form of argument. Right now, I will present it more formally, along with the example of external world sceptical thinking to make it easier to grasp.)

1 (a) Some *kind of potential knowledge* is highlighted (such as external world knowledge); (b) some *kind of evidence* (such as apparently observational evidence) is identified as being needed for having such knowledge.
2 We describe an inherent *limitation* on the power of (1b)'s kind of evidence. (For example, we accept that even one's apparently observational evidence could unwittingly be present as part of one's dreaming.)
3 We reinforce (2): we notice how the limitation described in (2) remains, *no matter how much* of (1b)'s kind of evidence is present. Hence that limitation on the evidence's power is qualitative, not quantitative: the limitation cannot be escaped by gathering *more* of the evidence. (For example, the dreaming possibility persists, no matter how much apparently observational evidence one has.)

4 We accept, independently, that no *other* kind of evidence could overcome that limitation described in (2) and (3), by supplanting or supplementing (1b)'s kind of evidence as a way to have (1a)'s kind of knowledge.

5 From (3) plus (4), we infer that an inescapable limitation afflicts the *only* possible way to use evidence to gain (1a)'s kind of knowledge (such as external world knowledge).

6 From (5), we conclude that there cannot be *any* instances of that kind of knowledge. (For example, external world scepticism is true.)

In effect, sceptical thinking denies that the *justification* component of our justified-true-belief theory of knowledge can be satisfied for the kind of knowledge being discussed. For instance, no apparently observational evidence can be strong enough for knowing the physical world – thanks to the dreaming possibility. Yet that sort of knowledge depends on that sort of evidence, and no other kind of evidence could overcome that limitation. Hence, there cannot be knowledge of the physical world. (In this section's spirit of generalization, by the way, note that even sceptical reasoning about external world knowledge need not be built around a possibility of dreaming. Think likewise of the possibility that you are hallucinating randomly, say, perhaps because your brain is misfiring without you or anyone else noticing. Or perhaps some alcohol or other drug is having a delayed and deluding effect on you, without you realizing this. And so on.)

5.4 Non-observational knowledge of one's not dreaming?

Armed with that general picture of sceptical thinking, we may revisit the Cartesian dreaming argument. It denies that one can ever know *observationally* that one is not dreaming. The argument infers that one can never know *at all* that one is not dreaming. But could you know *non*-observationally (using a different kind of evidence) that you are not dreaming?

Here are two suggestions.

Common sense. You might have been thinking that it is an affront to common sense to take seriously such an odd possibility. 'Nothing could be clearer to me than that I am seeing – *not* dreaming seeing – the world.' That is a natural reaction. How much philosophical impact should it have? Common-sense pronouncements are oft-used data within philosophy. Are they decisive? Or are they not philosophical enough to be engaging with the sceptical thinking? Are they 'talking past' the sceptical argument? In any event (the sceptical thinking might continue), could you be in a state of dreaming that affects your sense of what is commonsensical? Might you be *dreaming* your feeling of what is common-sense thinking?

Intuition. 'It remains *intuitively* clear to me that I am not dreaming. That is a powerful datum.' Even this might not be enough. We saw (section 4.7) how unhelpful it can be to rely on claims about intuition when philosophical ideas are in the air. Moreover, *is* what you call 'an intuition' genuinely non-observational? In claiming to report an intuition, you might rely, without noticing it, on what you have *observed* in your life – what you have seen and heard about how the world functions. In which case, you are *not* offering a non-observational response to the dreaming argument. You would still be within the clutches of that argument.

5.5 Brain-in-a-vat external world scepticism

The dreaming argument is not the only way of reasoning to an external world scepticism. Meet the *brain-in-a-vat* argument. It is like the dreaming argument, but is built around a more dramatic possibility.

Consider the thought that your brain is no longer inside your head, because it is floating in a vat of appropriate chemicals. (When you were asleep last night, it was abducted. Your body was left behind.) Your brain is now controlled by a sophisticated computer: there is a consciousness that *feels* to itself like it is you, perceiving the world normally. Yet that feeling is not being experienced by a normal human being, let alone by the normal human being (you) whom the consciousness *takes* itself to be. That brain in that vat is deeply deceived. It feels like it is you, sensing the world normally. But it has no evidence beyond what is generated within it by the computer. And none of that computer-generated evidence reveals the dire reality. The brain feels like it is seeing a normal world in a normal way; the computer is not allowing it to see the awful truth – that it is a disembodied brain in a vat.

You are thereby trapped, without realizing it. If you *are* a brain in a vat, this entrapment is physical: maybe *you* no longer even exist. Even if you are not a brain in a vat, you are still trapped. (But might the brain *itself* have knowledge, even if you-as-a-larger-being do not? Section 2.2.1 asked whether a brain *per se* could know something. Now that question gains added urgency.) You are trapped in an *epistemic* way: as a potential *knower*, you are unwittingly imprisoned. How so? No matter what apparently observational evidence you seem to have, it could be merely the computer's doing; and you cannot *know* (via the same sort of evidence, after all) that this is not happening to you, a brain in a vat being manipulated and deceived. You therefore lack all knowledge of your surroundings. At least, this is what the sceptical argument says.

5.6 Evil demon scepticism

Next we meet a famous argument for a wider-ranging
– indeed, a universal – scepticism. It denies us all knowledge, not only external world knowledge.

Imagine your beliefs being wholly controlled by
an evil demon, who is God-like in power, but Satan-
like in intent, towards your beliefs. You feel like you
are experiencing and thinking normally. But you are
deceived in having that feeling; the evil demon has
implanted it within you. The demon gives you false
beliefs whenever it chooses. The demon also adjusts
your experience and thinking so that you never notice
anything untoward. Hence, no demon-proof evidence is
available to you. Anything in your mind – any experience of which you are aware, any reasoning that you
might pursue – can be present because the demon put
it there. You are epistemically trapped, no matter how
free and powerful your mind feels to you. What is
12 x 13? '156', you reply. But even your capacity to
think mathematically could have been planted within
your mind by the demon. Any attempt by you to prove
mathematically your '156'-answer could also be the
demon's doing!

5.7 The *Cogito*

Like the dreaming argument (section 5.2), the evil
demon argument (section 5.6) comes from Descartes,
also in his 1641 'Meditation I'. Yet he was not a
sceptic. Even in that same book – *Meditations on
First Philosophy* – he did not end as a sceptic. Having
posed his evil demon sceptical challenge, he thought
that he could evade its sceptical conclusion. He con-
cluded, along the following lines, that he had some
knowledge which even an evil demon could not
spirit away.

> We have sought to imagine a demon with this special power: any thought within one's mind might be due to the demon's putting it there (a demon who is happy to be spreading *false* thoughts).
>
> Yet one cannot help but notice the thought's *existence* (regardless of whether it is false). Necessarily, one knows that it is present.
>
> One also cannot help but realize that any thought is being thought by *a thinker*, and that any thinker *exists* while thinking. So, if one knows that one is thinking, one knows that one *exists as* that thinker of that thought.

This move by Descartes is legendary within philosophy. He formulated it in Latin as 'cogito ergo sum': 'I think, therefore I am/exist.' So, people call it the *Cogito*. It appeared in Descartes's 'Meditation II', where he began trying to escape the sceptical traps that he had laid for himself in 'Meditation I'. Descartes claims that, even when being wholly suspicious of the origin and truth of his thoughts, he still knows *that he has them*. Thus, he knows that he is alive as that thinker at that moment.

This is a kind of self-knowledge. Knowledge like this – of what one's thoughts are, knowledge gained simply by 'looking within' – would be *introspective* knowledge. If it is available, universal scepticism is false: the evil demon will have been evaded!

5.8 Introspection scepticism

But was Descartes right to reject the evil demon sceptical argument by reaching for his *Cogito*?

Reflect further on the thought 'I am thinking' or even 'This – right now -- is some thinking'. These thoughts include words. Those words are from a language. (I have used English. Again, Descartes's *Cogito* was in Latin.) Any language includes rules, usually used correctly by competent speakers of the language: without such rules, there *is* no language. Yet if a language-rule can be used correctly, in principle it can be used incorrectly. So the possibility of mistake enters, potentially present even when introspecting to know one's thoughts. Mistake is an inescapable possibility, inherent in using language, even in reporting one's thoughts. Indeed, by introspecting 'in the privacy' of your own mind, there is an *increased* possibility of mistake (in formulation and interpretation): you cannot check with anyone else while purely introspecting.

Ludwig Wittgenstein, a highly influential twentieth-century Austrian philosopher, asked whether it is possible to use a 'private language' – usable only by oneself, answerable to no one else's authority. His answer was 'No, it is impossible' – because, *inescapably*, mistakes are possible when one tries to follow rules of language.

Thus, once more, sceptical reasoning pounces! Even the *Cogito* uses words. So, it depends for its meaning on a larger language, presumably a public one, which leaves it answerable in that respect to how other people use words. Descartes could have unwittingly been misusing words at that vital moment. Introspection cannot escape that limitation, even for thoughts like 'I am angry', 'I am sad', or 'I am in pain'. On this sceptical story, you never know even what is happening consciously inside your mind.

5.9 Other minds scepticism

If there can be sceptical doubts (such as in section 5.8) about knowing one's own mind, it might be even easier to raise sceptical doubts about knowing someone else's mind.

Can you literally observe another's thoughts and feelings? No. Can you observe her body, her actions ('yes') – and then know (by reasoning from those observations) that she has thoughts and feelings 'behind' those actions, often generating them? We talk of knowing aspects of another's mental life: 'I'm coming to know how she thinks. I'm learning her motivations. These are part of why I care about her.' The alternative sounds disturbing: 'I cannot know anyone else's having an inner life at all.'

Yet some sceptical thinking takes us in exactly that worrying alternative direction. Might the person beside you be a *zombie*, lacking feelings or thoughts? Could your own child be like that? Or your parents? Your spouse? Your friends? Could everyone else be like that? An *other minds sceptic* claims so. Must you forever fail to know other people as having mental lives at all? *Other minds scepticism* infers 'Yes!' That seems like an awful idea with which to live.

5.10 Scepticism about inductive knowledge

Other minds scepticism (section 5.9) perpetuates the prospect of there being inherent and substantial limits upon what knowledge we could ever gain from observation. Philosophy's history has discussed that limitation in various ways.

Welcome to *the problem of induction*. It was first formulated by the eighteenth-century Scottish philosopher David Hume (1711–76). He treated it as a scepticism about the rational nature and strength of *inductive* evidence (as we now call it).

Think of how often you form beliefs from observations that you *have* made, beliefs that you treat as knowledge of circumstances that you have *not* observed (and perhaps never will observe). Sometimes, this believing-beyond-observation is overt: 'The sun will rise tomorrow', 'The world existed long before it was ever observed', etc. Sometimes, the believing-beyond-observing is more subtle: 'That is a cat' (not the pedantic 'That is just a current time-slice – a here-and-now part – of what might be a longer-lived being, a possibly continuing-through-time cat'). In such cases, there are observations – plus a belief about something beyond those observations.

We can extend that characterization to more than a single person's observing at a single time. Let *observing* also encompass reading about others' observations, including ones that they have reported. A body of culturally or scientifically recorded experiences, for instance, can be absorbed within this broader category of observations. We might then hope that *much* extra knowledge will arise from such observations.

Even so (as Hume realized), a sceptical concern arises. No matter how many observations have occurred, and no matter how much sophisticated observational science has been done, it is always possible that *crucial* observations have not yet occurred. By 'crucial', I mean that these further possible observations might *conflict* seriously with whatever pattern of observations has actually arisen until now.

Thus (continues the sceptical argument), relying on observational evidence – even impressive experimental data gathered by good science – is inherently risky. This is so even if there have been many observations, and even if one has inferred from them only a *likelihood* (not a certainty) about what would be revealed by further observations. ('I'm saying only that it's probable, not that it's certain, that X will happen.') Perhaps one is about to experience a long run of observations that will conflict significantly even with whatever *probabilistic* pattern has so far been observed. You would have been mistaken, it will turn out, even in saying just that X would *probably* happen.

And (adds the sceptical argument) no non-observational alternative is available to help us here. You cannot know *non*-observationally that the sun will rise tomorrow. You cannot know *non*-observationally that a world existed before being observed. Inductive evidence has been vital, so far, for would-be knowers. This applies to personal knowledge of the world, historical knowledge, scientific knowledge of the skies and beyond, knowledge of one's character, and so on. If there is no inductive knowledge, it seems, we lack *so* much knowledge.

5.11 Memory scepticism

Inductive knowledge would not always be of the future. If available, it could often be of the *past*, including one's own past. So even this knowledge is at risk if we cannot evade inductive scepticism. When archaeologists extrapolate from fossil evidence to claims about animals from millions of years ago, they seem to be using induction. Are they gaining *knowledge* of the past? Universities fund them on the assumption that knowledge is indeed arising. But *is* it? And this worry spreads far beyond archaeology. If *it* is vulnerable to a scepticism about induction's ever delivering knowledge, so are many sciences.

Worse than that, those earlier sceptical worries about *external world* knowledge affect (along the following lines) memory's capacity to deliver knowledge.

Some of your thoughts feel to you like strong and vivid memories, hence excellent for knowing aspects of your past (such as what you did last summer).

Yet remembering is not merely a feeling. (It might not always involve a feeling at all; that is a separate point.) *Accuracy* is needed. Memory knowledge is like other knowledge in that way: truth is vital.

So, even when feeling that you are remembering well, you need to *corroborate* this with a different kind of knowledge – most obviously, observational knowledge. Otherwise, you cannot know that you are not relying on a *false* memory, such as a *mere* feeling of remembering well. (For example, you might just be *imagining* rather than remembering.)

Thus, having memory knowledge depends on support by *non*-memory knowledge – most obviously, observational knowledge.

In which case, there is no *pure* memory knowledge: corroboration by non-memory knowledge – most obviously, observational knowledge – is needed.

In which case, there cannot be any memory knowledge until the external world sceptical challenge is solved.

Memory knowledge also faces a sceptical challenge of its own. Can you imagine the world's having sprung into existence five minutes ago? Of course you can: it would not have looked different now from how it actually looks now! And part of what would have been created was all of us (you, me, everyone else) having the same memory feelings as we have, with most of them still seeming to be about events from more than five minutes ago. None of those about-longer-than-five-minutes-ago memory feelings would *really* be memories, though, since they would be false. Even now, therefore, do you lack memory knowledge until you know that the world was *not* created five minutes ago? Yet how *could* you know this? You cannot (says the sceptical reasoning).

5.12 Disagreement scepticism

Suppose that we have always *agreed* on a specific belief's being knowledge. Would this be enough to *make* the belief knowledge? Would the belief thereby evade sceptical arguments? This is not clear. Just as people can agree, they can disagree; even when they have not yet disagreed, maybe they will soon do so. It is possible that if some further idea was thrown into a conversation, existing agreement would unravel. Is *disagreement scepticism* another reason for regarding people as not knowing much?

We can make that question more precise with the idea of an *epistemic peer*. Your *social* peers have much the same social standing as you do. Your *financial* peers have much the same financial standing as you do. And your epistemic peers have much the same *epistemic* standing as you do. What does it mean in practice, then, when an epistemic peer disagrees with you? An epistemic peer on a given topic is as intelligent and thoughtful as you on that topic, with the same (or equivalent) evidence as you have, etc. If she disagrees with you, she is saying that you are mistaken. Does this automatically weaken your evidence? Must your claim therefore fail to be knowledge?

Here you are, with a particular belief. There she is, an epistemic peer on the same topic, rejecting your belief. What to do? What to say? Wait a moment; not only *you* face these questions. They apply equally to your epistemic peer. Because she disagrees with you, in effect you disagree with her. Is *her* evidence thus too weak to allow *her* belief to be knowledge? Should *both* you and she suspend your competing beliefs, until the disagreement is resolved? Would both you and she lack knowledge, due to this disagreement? A sceptic can say so.

Of course, how often do you actually find yourself disagreeing with an epistemic peer on a topic? It might be rare. But what of the *possibility* of its happening? Is it always possible (even when you feel like your evidence is excellent) that someone just as intelligent, thoughtful, and intellectually careful will disagree with you?

And what of the possibility of disagreeing with yourself? Perhaps you-at-a-later-time will disagree with you-now, reacting to the same evidence. Or maybe you-at-a-later-time could have better evidence, and will regard you-now as having weaker evidence. Hence, should you concede already that none of your present beliefs are knowledge? Perhaps evidence currently in your mind should not stay there; can you know now that no better, and conflicting, evidence awaits – evidence that should cause you to revise your current thinking? A sceptic may deny that you can ever properly rule out this possibility.

5.13 Replying to sceptical arguments

What is the epistemological significance of sceptical arguments? If correct, they reveal something striking about our minds' limited capacities: namely, we know much less than we think we do.

But what if sceptical arguments are not correct? Even then, they might matter. When epistemologists value sceptical arguments, this need not be due to being personally convinced by the arguments. Few epistemologists call themselves 'sceptics'. Still, many allow that engaging with sceptical arguments can help us to think more deeply about the nature of knowing. The rest of this chapter mentions a few ideas that might emerge from such thinking.

5.13.1 Knowing contextually

It is often thought that most, maybe all, sceptical reasoning *imposes irrelevantly high standards* upon would-be knowers. Of course, any sceptic would disagree: 'No, you *should* be able to know that you are not dreaming, if you are to know the world around you. If you are dreaming, the world might not *really* be as it *appears* to you.' So, what is meant by saying that sceptical standards are irrelevantly high? The idea could be that a *merely* possible reason for doubt is being posited. The thought that one *could* be dreaming rarely, if ever, feels like a *real* reason to doubt oneself.

How can we make progress on that potential impasse? How should we decide whether sceptical arguments succeed? No sure-fire way of answering this question to everyone's satisfaction has emerged. It is one of *the* most energetically debated epistemological questions.

Some epistemologists urge us to focus on how people *talk* about knowing. Notice how readily, in different conversational contexts, people can *shift* between quite varying standards for allowing or denying knowledge:

> *Normal setting.* 'Do you know what that is?' 'Yes, it's a zebra.' 'Thanks.'
>
> *Less-normal setting.* 'Do you know what that is?' 'Yes, it's a zebra.' 'Hmm. Might it be a mule that has been painted to look like a zebra?' 'Well, that's possible.' 'So, you don't know that it isn't a disguised mule?' 'I suppose not. I hadn't thought about it. And I haven't stood close enough to the animal to check on this.' 'Then you don't really know that it's a zebra?' 'Perhaps not.'

Puzzling! In the normal setting, knowledge is readily attributed, presumably by applying a normal standard for knowing. But in the less-normal setting, that seems not to occur. In that context, is a *higher* standard for knowing being applied? And does a setting *become* less normal when a sceptical possibility (such as that one is dreaming) is mentioned in a serious tone of voice? Is one suddenly obliged to respect that odd idea, in a way that also – perhaps suddenly – makes sceptical reasoning relevant?

That point favours sceptical doubts, by suggesting that there *can* be contexts where sceptical talk sounds appropriate. How far does the point extend, though? *Contextualism* is a recent approach within epistemology. Contextualists talk about how we talk about knowing. They claim that this can help us to find the appropriate limits of sceptical reasoning. In normal settings, maybe we can rightly be said to know. But contextualists accept that there are settings – perhaps special ones created when a sceptical possibility is mentioned seriously – where we no longer apply those normal standards for knowing: in those settings, we *can* rightly be denied knowledge, in light of sceptical possibilities. When the disguised-mules possibility is suggested, for example, suddenly one might feel that one does *not* know that the animal is a zebra – 'because yes, I suppose that I do *not* know that it is not a disguised mule'.

Yet contextualists generally do not see themselves as sceptics. They offer the following advice. When attributing knowledge normally, looking for standard signs of knowing (such as good evidence), continue doing so. Confront sceptical concerns only when they arise naturally in thought or talk. When they do, you might rightly deny knowledge, even to yourself (such as by conceding that you do not know of your not dreaming). But (and here is the main anti-sceptical suggestion) even this concession to sceptical concerns need not affect your using the word 'know' in *other* contexts. Even if it is right for you to deny knowledge when a sceptical possibility arises, you still need not deny knowledge when you are in a *normal* context. We may *quarantine* sceptical conclusions, restricting their applicability to those scarce settings where sceptical possibilities have been mentioned seriously. Elsewhere, they pose no threat.

5.13.2 Knowing fallibly

Perhaps progress could also be made by distinguishing between *fallible knowledge* and *infallible knowledge*.

Knowing something infallibly disposes rationally of *every possible* doubt about its being true. Knowing something fallibly leaves open at least a *possibility* of one's belief being mistaken – even while being knowledge.

So, is it possible to know something fallibly? You might say, 'I know that Donald Trump is President of the US. My evidence for this is *good enough*, even if not literally *perfect*. There is always a *possibility* of being mistaken. So what, though? *Good enough* evidence is part of knowing *well enough* that he is President. This is all that is ever needed, for action, for living.'

What should a concept of fallible knowledge look like? We might turn our justified-true-belief theory of knowledge (from section 4.6) into something like the following, by adding the final clause ('and without ...'):

Knowing = Having a true belief that is well justified – but not in any way that is too like what happens within some Gettier case, and without the justification's *guaranteeing* the belief's being true.

On this fallibilist picture, a true belief can be knowledge via evidence that provides *good enough, even if not perfect,* support for the belief's being true.

And if there can be knowledge like that, then (we might say) knowing would not always *require* one to do enough to satisfy the higher justificatory standard imposed by sceptical arguments. Feel free to want to satisfy that standard. But *need* you satisfy it, if you are to have knowledge? Or it is possible to fall short of satisfying it, while having *good enough* evidence and hence *fallible* knowledge? Maybe all human knowledge is fallible. (Might humans be forever fallible in whatever we do?)

Even if that is so, epistemology could still retain an idea of infallible knowledge as an ideal. Even if only

God could have infallible knowledge, we might really care to understand what God's knowing would involve, as part of understanding God's nature. Do sceptical arguments speak to a desire sometimes to be *more* than human – to know something perfectly? If we find ourselves trapped by sceptical thinking, can this be because we are hoping – forlornly? – to know in that exalted way? Maybe sceptical arguments show only that *we* cannot know as *God* knows.

5.13.3 Knowing in more or less depth

I gestured just now at a concept of knowledge-fallibilism. The aim is to understand what it would be to know something in a humanly realistic way. Let us paint one picture of what knowing fallibly could involve.

People often talk of knowing a *topic* in greater or lesser depth. Can a *particular fact* be known in greater or lesser depth? A topic includes facts. Can a fact include further facts? The eighteenth-century English poet William Blake (in 'Auguries of Innocence') wrote this:

> To see a World in a Grain of Sand
> And a Heaven in a Wild Flower
> Hold Infinity in the palm of your hand
> And Eternity in an hour

Is something like that possible for knowing a fact? Might there be such depth in knowing a fact?

When someone claims to know 'That's a barn', for instance, she claims knowledge of an aspect of reality. She *sums up* this knowledge with words apparently reporting a single fact: 'That's a barn.' But this fact is constituted by further facts, its 'contained' details. That is a barn; *how* is it a barn? Specific pieces of wood are arranged thus-and-so; particular nails are used; etc.

'Deeper' facts underlie those ones, interlinking them, such as laws of woodwork, of engineering, even of physics. Perhaps social facts contribute, so that this is a barn and not an art installation. All of these are facts 'within' that first fact, collectively summed up as 'That's a barn.' A fact can thus include further facts, as a topic can include facts. In this sense, a fact often *is* a topic.

This *metaphysical* complexity within a fact suggests part of an *epistemological* picture of knowing that fact: one might know the fact partly by knowing facts 'within' it. In knowing that an object is a barn, one might know some of those further facts mentioned a moment ago – because they are 'within' the fact being known (the fact that the object is a barn).

An intriguing question arises. Could a fact, such as 'That's a barn', be known in more – or in less – *depth*? This would be one's knowing more, or knowing fewer, of those facts (those further details) embedded within that fact ('That's a barn'). This might occur in various ways, to differing extents. The farmer who owns the barn could know the fact that the object is a barn more fully than you know it. A structural engineer can also know that fact more fully than you do, yet in a different way from how the farmer does: each knows different further facts within the fact of the object's being a barn. You might know in an 'everyday' way that the object is a barn. So there is flexibility and plurality here. We can portray different people, or one person at different times, as knowing the same fact in different ways: various strengths and depths of knowledge are possible, even for knowledge of a particular fact.

We may combine that suggestion with our justified-true-belief theory. Setting aside for now (and for simplicity) section 5.13.2's addition of an explicitly fallibilist condition to that theory, we could have something like this:

(1) Knowing = Having a true belief that is well
    justified – but not in any way that is too like
    what happens within some Gettier case.
(2) Knowing a fact F can include further knowing,
    of facts *within* F – with all of this knowledge
    satisfying (1).

Clause (1) is what we already had: it is our basic
justified-true-belief theory. It describes *non*-knowledge
elements joining together to constitute knowledge. This
is like understanding an elephant's nature in standard
biological terms.
    Clause (2) is new. It describes how an instance of
knowing, after being constituted in (1)'s way, might
include further instances of knowing. This is like saying
that, after many months of gestation, a particular elephant includes another elephant within her. Each is an
elephant by satisfying those standard biological terms.
But one of them is also partly constituted at that moment,
as the particular elephant that she is, by including the
other elephant. If we do not understand this, we do not
understand her elephant-nature fully at that moment.
    On the suggested picture, knowing is always more or
less detailed or full in its engagement with a fact F. Any
knowing of F '*burrows*' more, or less, deeply into the
range of facts 'within' F (whatever facts are joining
together to constitute F). So, F is being known more – or
less – deeply, depending on *how many of the constitu-
tively significant facts within* F are being known.

5.13.4 Knowing versus knowing that one knows

Section 5.13.2 proposed the possibility of knowing a
fact *fallibly*. Section 5.13.3 suggested that knowing a
fact always occurs more, or less, *deeply*, as we 'burrow'

more, or less, fully into the fact's 'inner' constitutive details. Do those two ideas now provide a way to evade scepticism's potentially grim clutches?

Let us imagine a conversation on this issue. It will focus on one of history's most influential scepticisms – the Cartesian dreaming argument about external world knowledge.

> *Non-sceptic*   I know that my friend entered the room a moment ago. (There she is, listening to us with interest.)
>
> *Sceptic*   No, you don't really know it. You *believe* that she entered the room (and that you see her now). You take yourself to have good evidence in support of that belief, because you feel that you *saw* her enter. *But you might have been dreaming*, hence not actually seeing her. So, what you think is *good observational evidence* of her entering the room is nothing of the sort.
>
> *Non-sceptic*   But you are forgetting that knowledge can be fallible. I'm happy to admit that I do not have perfect or infallible knowledge of my friend's entering the room; I'm only human. What I claim is *fallible* knowledge of her entering the room. That is *good enough* as knowledge. And it doesn't require me to have *evidence* so good as to eliminate even the possibility of my dreaming. My evidence is *good enough*, even if not perfect.
>
> *Sceptic*   Unfortunately you're misjudging the nature, and hence strength, of the dreaming possibility. It applies to (and weakens) *all* would-be observational evidence. You can't have even *fallible* knowledge, because you can't have even *good* observational evidence.
>
> *Non-sceptic*   Okay, that's your reply to the suggestion (section 5.13.2) that knowledge can be fallible. You're saying that even fallible knowledge involves good evidence – but that I lack even good observational evidence, thanks to the ever-hovering dreaming possibility. I realize that the dreaming possibility is meant to apply to *all* seemingly observational evidence. If I'm to evade your scepticism, then, I need

something more than the general claim that fallibility can be part of knowing. Somehow I have to neutralize the dreaming possibility, so that it isn't turning every instance of would-be observational evidence into no-real-evidence-at-all!

Sceptic That's right.

Non-sceptic Then let's consider the other suggestion that we met (in section 5.13.3) when thinking about fallibility – namely, the 'burrowing' picture of knowing. Are you also saying that I can't know my friend's entering the room by knowing enough of the facts 'within' that fact about her (those 'smaller' facts that combine to constitute – to *be*, collectively – the fact of her entering the room)? I'm tempted to claim that I can know *well enough* that she has entered the room, by knowing *enough* of those 'inner' facts, even if I don't also know the I-am-not-dreaming fact. But you're denying that I could be helped by this move, right? You're saying that I can't know *any* of those 'inner' facts *until* I have knowledge that disposes directly of the I-am-dreaming possibility?

Sceptic Yes, that's so. Any attempt to know enough of those 'inner' facts (the ones 'within' the fact of your friend's entering the room) remains subject to the dreaming possibility: you could be dreaming *their* being facts. In that way, the I-am-not-dreaming fact stands 'apart' from those others (the ones that would be 'within' the fact of your friend's entering the room). Unlike them, it would not be *part* of the fact of your friend entering the room.

Non-sceptic. Aha, that is what I wanted to hear! Now I'm confident that I do have a powerful reply to you. Now I can show that you face a different problem for motivating your sceptical thinking. And I *can* show this by using that second proposal (from section 5.13.3), the knowing-a-fact-by-burrowing-into-it picture.

Sceptic Really? How could that be so?

Non-sceptic You said just now that the I-am-not-dreaming fact would not be *part* of the fact of my friend's entering the room. That sounds reasonable: the I-am-not-dreaming fact is about me, while the other fact is about her. But let's think about which 'larger' fact *does* literally include the I-am-not-dreaming fact about me. The answer is very revealing.

Sceptic   Why? How? What does it reveal?

Non-sceptic   It shows that you are confusing two kinds or 'levels' of knowing.

Sceptic   I doubt that.

Non-sceptic   Well, here's my argument. (Please bear with me. It's complex. I'll present it in four steps.)

1 Why is the I-am-not-dreaming fact mentioned by the sceptical reasoning? The reason is that it has a potentially *related* role: it would be a fact 'within' a potentially related fact. What would that other fact be? Hopefully, it is the fact of my *apparently* good observational evidence's being *actually* good observational evidence (of my friend's entering the room). *This* is why I might want to not be only dreaming my apparently observational evidence. I want the I-am-not-dreaming fact to literally be a *part* of my apparently observational evidence's being actually observational, and hence being actually good evidence. (The evidence would be actually good because, in part, it is not actually being dreamt.)

2 In that way, however, the I-am-not-dreaming fact would also be a fact within my *knowing* that my friend has entered the room. For part of my *having* this knowledge would be my having *actually* good observational evidence of my friend's entering the room. And part of my having that *actually* good observational evidence of her entering the room would, in turn, be my *not actually dreaming* of her entering the room. (If my apparently good observational evidence is not being dreamt, it is that much *closer* to being actually good observational evidence.)

3 So, when you claim that I need to know that I'm not dreaming (if I'm to know my friend's having

entered the room), you're saying the following. You're saying that I need to know a particular fact – the I-am-not-dreaming fact – that would literally be a *part* of my knowing observationally that my friend has entered the room. That is, literally a part of my knowing (via real observation) that she has entered the room is my *not merely dreaming* that she has done so.

4 Thus, you're asking me to have some particular knowledge – the I-am-not-dreaming knowledge – that would (on the suggested 'burrowing' picture of knowing) be knowledge of a fact (I-am-not-dreaming) *within my knowing* that my friend has entered the room. And, with this realization, we have uncovered the real role that would be played by my knowing that I am not dreaming! It would be my *knowing that* my apparently good observational evidence is actually good observational evidence (because I am not dreaming it). Hence, it would be my *knowing that I pass at least that test for knowing* that my friend has entered the room.

Sceptic Well, why should I be worried by that implication?

Non-sceptic It means that you're confused in a key way when insisting on my needing to know that I am not dreaming. You're running together two important ideas that should be kept apart when trying to understand what is involved in knowing something.

Sceptic Hmm. Could you please be more specific?

Non-sceptic Of course. You're confusing *knowing* F with *knowing that one knows* F. You've confused my knowing that my friend has entered the room, with my knowing *about that knowing*. You've confused my knowing that she has entered, with my knowing *that I know* that she has entered. That is a confusion because in principle I could know about my friend *without* knowing anything about knowing at all – let alone about this particular knowing about her! Suppose that I had never thought about the nature of knowledge. Surely I could still know about my friend, without having in mind even the *concepts* of good evidence and knowledge.

Sceptic Are you saying that I've turned your knowing about your friend into something more complicated and intellectual than it needs to be?

Non-sceptic Yes! Isn't it often possible to know something more simply, without *knowing that* one knows it – that is, without knowing *about* the knowing? Epistemologists speak of the KK-principle, which says that *Knowing* something has to include *Knowing that one Knows it.* (For short: K must include KK.) This is a contentious principle. So, the failing I've now described is that your sceptical argument requires *all* knowing to include reflection *on* knowing – on one's own knowing, at least. This is highly unrealistic. Yes, some knowing is like that (when people are being self-reflective). Yet why should *all* knowing be so? This is how the dreaming argument sets an irrelevantly high standard for knowing in general.

Here is a simple way to remember that non-sceptical point: we might distinguish between *animal* knowledge of a fact F and *reflective* knowledge of F. Earlier (section 2.2.5), we asked whether non-human animals ever know, as we seem to know. Now we can ask whether people ever know, as non-human animals seem to know. Are there at least those two '*levels*' of knowing – the animal and the reflective? Could a single fact (such as someone's entering a room) be known in either an animal way *or* a reflective way? The non-sceptical argument given just now concludes that sceptical reasoning impugns *at most* our having reflective knowledge – and that we are confused if we think of such reasoning as threatening *all* attempts to know.

With that said, I do not offer these non-sceptical suggestions as being unanswerably correct. Sceptical arguments have long sparked counter-suggestions that strive to learn from those arguments without being overcome by them. It is wise not to be too insistently non-sceptical. Again, few epistemologists accept sceptical conclusions. But even if you reject those conclusions, you might hope to do it more thoughtfully and insightfully: you can try to *diagnose* what goes awry within arguments for those sceptical conclusions. This remains a challenge within epistemology.

6

Applying Epistemology

6.1 Can we apply our epistemology?

Earlier chapters have encouraged us to be epistemological *builders*, constructing and refining theories of knowledge, hopefully reaching an accurate theory of knowledge. But accuracy is one thing; usefulness is another. We should also want our theory of knowledge to help us in how we *live*. Let us therefore spend a little time as epistemological *judges*, confronting several 'real world' questions in light of our theory of knowledge and its concepts.

The next three sections present an array of humanly significant questions. Each question is followed by a brief argument and counter-argument, inspired and shaped partly by epistemological ideas. Always, the challenge is to respond in a reasoned way, adverting to those competing ideas. (Sometimes, the argument and counter-argument advocate literally a 'yes' and then a 'no.' Sometimes, they are just alternative lines of thought. Sometimes, the epistemology involved is explicit; at times, it is implicit.) Please treat these as spirited conversations to which you are welcome to contribute.

Each time, what do *you* think about the issue? Each time, how can you apply *epistemology* to it? Being epistemological will not automatically tell you what to think about yourself, life, and the world. But it can *improve* that thinking.

6.2 Self-knowledge questions

Descartes's *Cogito* (section 5.7) was a classic claim to self-knowledge: 'I think, therefore I am.' But it is not overtly practical self-knowledge. These days, most of what we call 'self-knowledge' bears more *manifestly* upon major practical questions within our lives – what to think about oneself, what to do with oneself. This section presents three such questions – Being a Good Person, Loving Someone, and Having a Life Plan.

6.2.1 Being a good person

Question. 'I'm a good person. I'm not perfect; I'm the first to admit that. Fundamentally, though, I'm good. I have an inner core of moral goodness.' Versions of this claim are often made or thought, it seems. But are such claims ever reporting *knowledge* of one's basic goodness? *Can* one know that, in some inner fundamental way, one is a good person?

Being a good person: argument. Thankfully, I *can* know that I'm a good person – not perfect, but good. I need only introspect – 'using my mind to look into itself' – to know what I'm like as a person, at least in such important and defining respects. What could be simpler? No one could have better evidence on this than I do. Even if others sometimes observe me acting badly 'in the world', that is not decisive. Only I can know how I am 'within myself'; and only this is decisive for how I 'really' am, especially in my ultimate moral nature. After all, 'within myself' is where my being a good person is constituted, where it *exists*. So I pause, focusing calmly, reflecting briefly; and lo – I can know enough of my intentions and emotions, enough of what and how I think and feel. And this is enough for knowing my ultimate moral character, my inner goodness. Do I see inner perfection? No, because I notice some thoughts and feelings that a perfectly good person would probably lack. Still, I do see a reassuring kind and degree of goodness. It is part of me.

Being a good person: counter-argument. To call oneself 'good' (meaning 'morally good' or 'of morally good character') without knowing what, *in general*, such goodness is would be empty. (Or wishful thinking. Or bravado. Or arrogance.) It might feel reassuring to call oneself 'good' in spite of not knowing what goodness is in general. Yet feeling reassured is not the same as knowing. And knowledge that one is good is *not* gained by just 'looking within'. Knowing that one is good – even imperfectly good – includes knowing much *outside* oneself. Since it needs to be knowledge of what goodness is in general, it must include wide-ranging knowledge of human nature, of history, of psychology, and more besides. And there is no guarantee that one *will* ever have such extensive and complex knowledge: one might fall *far* short of having enough of the knowledge required to know even that one is 'not perfect, but good anyway'. For example, without much knowledge of human nature, history, psychology, and so on, one might not know what feelings one *should* have in various circumstances. Equally, one might not know what thoughts one *should* have about lots of actual and possible situations, in order to be reacting as a genuinely good person. One can hope and believe that one is good, without knowing that one is. Is it really up to each of us to make the ultimate determination of our own moral goodness? No, it is much more difficult than that: it is a more objective process, for a start! (This use of the term 'objective', by the way, is not imposing upon you a need for rational *certainty* if you are to know that you are a good person. It is saying that you need a particular *kind* – not a special *degree* – of evidence. Being good as a person is constituted partly by how one fits into, or compares with, relevant aspects of the world outside oneself. So, being a good person is not knowable without a comparatively 'outer' perspective on that wider world. This might include your needing to know yourself *from* the 'perspective' of the enveloping world – perhaps seeing yourself as well-informed others see you.)

6.2.2 Loving someone

Question. 'I love you.' This can be one of the most emotionally important and even life-changing thoughts that one ever has, or utterances that one ever makes. But how would one know that it is true?

Loving someone: argument. Love is a feeling. Hence, I need only *introspect* – 'looking within' – to know whether I am in love. Particularly so, because love is such a strong and distinctive feeling. I could never *mistakenly* be seeming to notice that feeling within me: for example, I could not confuse it with another feeling. Nor could I ever *overlook* entirely its being there. And because love is inescapably an emotion, this automatically places it beyond the reach of rational *criticism*. Yet, given the kind and strength of emotion that it is, love is entirely *knowable*, even in a wholly rational way. I accept that emotions can come and go, and that love can be fleeting. Thus, memory can be needed to know one's being in love *over* time. But whenever it is genuinely present, it remains obviously knowable. If it lasts for a long time, therefore, one has many such moments, maybe a single very lengthy 'moment', even most of a lifetime's 'moment'. A welcome state indeed, and knowably so!

Loving someone: counter-argument. First, perhaps love is a *complex* feeling. Even if you could easily recognize and know part of it, maybe further parts – elusive parts – are not easily recognizable. Could an infatuation, for example, be mistaken for love? Second, perhaps love is not just a feeling anyway. It might be able to be *overturned* quite rationally by new evidence: if you discover that your partner is a neo-Nazi, could that rationally be the end of your love for him or her? Love might also be not just a feeling, by being partly a *prediction*, maybe about feelings and actions. ('I feel like this, and *I will still do so* in twenty years' time. *I will still act* loyally and lovingly at that time.') So, even knowing now that one is in love would include knowing the future: it would be partly *inductive* knowledge, based predictively on past and present observations, such as of the other person. But there is a realistic possibility that the people involved will change significantly – including in ways that will extinguish the love – between now and later. If so, then even knowing (inductively) now that one is in love might be impossible. As to the idea of having *long* known one's being in love, excellent – except one should not forget how fallible memory can be! So, even one's supposedly excellent inductive evidence, of those many welcome memories of life with one's beloved, could be less secure evidence than they seem. Can't one be kidding oneself, without realizing it, about one's past feelings? Can't one be remembering selectively, somehow overlooking the evidence *against* one's having been in love over those past weeks, months, or years? It might be comforting to feel so purely that one has long been in love. However, even feeling comforted like that might fall short of having real knowledge.

6.2.3 Having a life plan

Question. 'What should I do with my life? I know: I should [do X; become a Y].' This is another significant thought that can define one's life. It would be better for such a thought to be knowledge when possible, rather than ... something lesser. Yet how does one have this knowledge?

Having a life plan: argument. I know my current preferences – what I like and value. I know what seems as though it would fit well with those preferences. All of this is clear to me because I remember my past experiences and how they affected me, I have listened to other people talking about life's opportunities, I have read widely about many professions and countries, I have talked with people familiar with me. All of this is excellent evidence. It gives me knowledge of the best paths for my life to tread.

Having a life plan: counter-argument. Here are two points.

1 Those preferences might only be current ones. Yet a choice of profession can shape one's life for years, during which time one might change fundamentally as a person. Do you know now – inductively – what will be good for you in the future? (A small example: knowing, when 20 years old, that a tattoo looks good on one does not guarantee knowing that it will look good when one is 40, or 50, etc.)

2 Knowing even one's current preferences might not be easy. Other people are not infallible guides as to one's character and talents. Someone advising you might unwittingly be 'projecting onto' you her own values and desires. (Why would *she* – unlike you – have inductive knowledge of what will be best for you? Inductive scepticism, we saw, concerns all extrapolation from experience. Hence, it applies even to people

with much more experience than you have had.) It is also easy to overlook how merely conventional, purely fashionable, ideas could be shaping your (and other people's) thinking, in ways that you will regret in later years. (It is not only *clothing* 'fashion choices' that can be embarrassing, years later.) This is a reason not to trust one's current evidence, even when it is observational and about oneself.

6.3 Moral-knowledge questions

Some personally important beliefs are overtly about moral matters: call these 'moral-beliefs'. When, if ever, are they moral-knowledge? People are persecuted, and wars are fought, in the name of moral-knowledge. But might there be no such knowledge? Can feelings of having it be illusory? Let us think about three questions with the potential to plunge us into life-or-death issues: Death Penalty, Abortion, and Not Being Racist.

6.3.1 Death penalty

Question. 'All else being equal, the death penalty is warranted when we know, beyond all reasonable doubt, that the defendant committed a terrible crime. And there *are* times when we have such knowledge.' How good is that reasoning?

Death penalty: argument. Criminal trials have rules of evidence and procedure. A verdict of 'guilty' reflects those rules being followed. The verdict is therefore knowledge of the defendant's guilt. More fully, the verdict, if true, is a *very* well justified true belief in that guilt. So much so, that the trial will have eliminated *all reasonable doubt*, thereby generating *infallible* knowledge of the guilt. Hence, the verdict *must* be true. Thus, the death penalty is at least not epistemologically suspect.

Death penalty: counter-argument. First, there are many epistemologically describable ways for an innocent person to mistakenly be deemed 'guilty'.

- Perhaps the police evidence includes significant falsity.
- Perhaps the police evidence overlooks (even deliberately so, if the associated police are corrupt) some vital facts.
- Perhaps the defence lawyer is incompetent, presenting the case poorly, such as by failing to notice those two previous possible failings in the evidence.
- Perhaps the prosecuting lawyer is far more skilled (and more highly paid), using rhetoric that misleads the jurors and obscures the evidence's failings.
- Perhaps the judge, maybe a juror or two, is badly inattentive out.
- Perhaps the judge, maybe a juror or two, is prejudiced against a community (such as a racial or ethnic one) to which the defendant belongs, perhaps distrusting members of that community as not being generally truthful.

And so on. The trial process includes much potential for fallibility. This is especially true when a defendant cannot afford good legal representation – as often happens.

Second, in recent years some convicted people, including death row inmates, have had their cases re-examined; often, the result has been a discovery of their innocence. (Read about the work done by The Innocence Project and, more generally, The Innocence Network, across many countries, but especially in the USA.) All too often, someone is convicted after a shoddy legal process, which can include available DNA evidence being ignored. How could this reflect intellectual virtue on the part of those who turn their back upon that evidence? And spare a thought for people who have been executed, yet who were innocent and who received poor legal treatment: the death penalty has not been applied only to actually guilty people. This is striking observational evidence: it gives us an epistemologically describable reason to doubt the death penalty's morality, certainly when that penalty is applied within a legal system run by people who are fallible (as, indeed, all of us are).

6.3.2 Abortion

Question. 'Even an early-pregnancy abortion is morally wrong.' Can this be known?

Abortion: argument. I know that killing an innocent person is morally wrong. I know that even an early-pregnancy embryo or foetus is a person – an innocent person. I know that to abort an embryo or foetus is to kill it. So, I know that even an early-pregnancy abortion is morally wrong. (I cannot know anything better or more strongly than I know these truths.)

Abortion: counter-argument. If that argument is so strong, the following argument should not be – and yet it is!

> I know that it is morally wrong to force an innocent woman to use her body in a way in which she does not want to use it. I know that not allowing a woman to have an early-pregnancy abortion is forcing her to use her body in a way in which she does not want to use it. So, I know that not allowing a woman to have an early-pregnancy abortion is morally wrong.

Consider the following point, too. Many people claim to know that an embryo or a foetus is a person. But many others *deny* that those people know an embryo or foetus to be a person: 'Even a strongly held belief is not therefore knowledge.' So, there is *disagreement* about whether people know that an embryo or a foetus is a person. Still, *no one* denies that we know that women are people. Thus, our evidence for women being people is *at least that much better* than for embryos or foetuses being people. And we should want our morality to be shaped by better rather than lesser evidence. Wherever there is better evidence, knowledge is more likely to be; and morality should be informed by knowledge.

6.3.3 Not being racist

Question. 'I'm not racist. I do not act in racist ways.' How can this be known? Most of us *want* this sort of knowledge about ourselves.

Not being racist: argument. I act well – considerately, amiably – towards people from other racial or ethnic backgrounds. I have no disrespectful attitudes towards those racial or ethnic backgrounds.

Not being racist: counter-argument. Consider these three points.

1 One might not have acted as well as one thinks that one has done during one's life. Memory can be very fallible, especially when one seems to remember having acted *well*. This could be a self-serving 'fake memory'.
2 It might be difficult to know that one is not reacting, without realizing it, to someone's racial or ethnic background. For example, one can think that one is objecting to a person's rudeness. Yet one might be misreading, as rudeness, what is just a culturally different style of talking. (Is this a more realistic cousin of the sceptical dreaming worry, that one can be dreaming even when feeling like one is observing normally?)
3 It is possible to act in ways that are unconsciously racist in 'larger' ways – *socially* constituted ways that

one has never noticed, and from which one has not 'escaped'. Actions by a socially privileged person could unthinkingly reflect and enact that privilege. Even *being in a position* – having the opportunity – to perform those actions might be due to one's social privilege, without one's being aware of this. People do not always see the *evidence* – which is, in a sense, all around them – of their privilege. This is reason to doubt that they could *know* when their actions are not racist, for instance. The point is that 'looking within', consulting 'inner' feelings and thoughts, will not give one knowledge of not somehow being racist. Someone might unwittingly be perpetuating a wider racism from around them, perhaps subtly enveloping them, unless they actively strive to escape its influence. (Is this *also* a more realistic cousin of the Cartesian sceptical dreaming worry that one is dreaming without noticing it?)

6.4 World-knowledge questions

As our lives take shape, we generally seek and claim practically significant knowledge of the wider world – a *much* wider world. This section focuses on four questions – God, History, Society, and Science – about what we might call 'world-knowledge'.

6.4.1 God

Question. 'There is a God – an infinitely good, knowing, and powerful being, who is ultimately responsible for creating and maintaining the world, all that there is.' How can something so momentous be known?

God: argument. I introspect, finding myself 'in touch' with God. I listen to socially respected authorities, who assure me that God exists. I read a holy book, often and carefully: it is holy because there is a God, and its testimony conveys so much that clearly flows from there being a God. I observe the world's order and majesty, which can be present only because of a supreme creator – God. I infer, from there being morally good actions and morally bad actions, that there is a God whose approval makes an action morally good or morally bad. I infer that, given this finite observable world, there must be something infinite and unobservable *beyond* it. Otherwise, there cannot be an underlying explanation of the finite and observable world. And that is impossible, because there *must* be some such explanation; I know this by pure *reason*.

God: counter-argument. I will respond to those claims in turn.

1 The fact that many people say that there is a God, or that some book is holy, does not ensure their being correct. Many others disagree with them about this. So we have a stand-off, between groups endorsing/ rejecting a position.

2 Even if the world is orderly (and majestic, in our view), perhaps that is simply what any world would be like if it was to exist. But this is no proof that it was *created* as orderly. Interpreting one's observations of the world as a whole is surely quite fallible.

3 In his dialogue *Euthyphro*, Plato famously described a fundamental problem with saying that an action is morally good because a God approves of it. In general, approval can be arbitrary, reflecting a mere whim. What really matters here is whether an action has been approved of by a God because it has features that *make* it good – thereby making it *worthy* of a God's approval. Any explanation of an action's moral goodness must look first to the action itself and its features, and only afterwards (if ever) to whether an external being, such as a God, approves of the action. So, one needs to know the nature of the action first,

presumably by observing it, before inferring from this that a God would approve of it. Would this knowledge of a God, even if possible, thus be inductive and fallible – reasoning from observations to an hypothesis about how a God would react? (And is this an hypothesis about an 'other mind' – a God's?)

4 On the supposed need for there to be an infinite and unobservable something existing beyond this finite and observable reality, well, what *if* there is no underlying explanation of this? Why must there be an explanation? Simply saying that one knows it through pure reason is not rationally decisive.

None of this proves that there is no God. But it suggests that, at best, we would know only fallibly of God's existing. We could at least not know infallibly of God – that is, with a certainty admitting of no rational doubt.

6.4.2 History

Question. 'Can we ever know the past – the "big" past, on a scale that historians study? For example, can we know that Nazi Germany oversaw a Jewish Holocaust in World War II?' Distressingly, some people deny us this knowledge. Does epistemology imply that we should respect what they say about this – 'because they *might* be right'?

History: argument. When trying to uncover what happened in a war that ended long ago, historians use *so* much data. They choose which data to retain and which to discard. They interpret it as best they can. What results is a theory, an historical interpretation. In general, however, when a theory arises from complex data, there can be competing theories for those same data. Even the supposed gas chambers in Nazi concentration camps have been claimed, by some authors, not to have been used for the mass killing of Jews in World War II. (It has been said, for instance, that the chambers were used just for killing lice on the prisoners.) The usual view, saying that mass killings of Jews did occur in those chambers, is thus not epistemically *mandatory*: the evidence does not *require* us to believe the usual interpretation. Historical knowledge is only ever historical 'knowledge'. Opinions differ. Even scholars – expert epistemic peers on this topic – can disagree with each other.

History: counter-argument. That reasoning reminds us only of something that any responsible historian already knows – namely, that any large-scale historical knowledge is fallible. But so what? Yes, there are always alternative *possible* interpretations of data. This does not make all possible interpretations *equally well supported* by the data, though. Historians are supposed to assess the respective strengths of potentially competing bodies of evidence, without simply assuming that these must be equally good! As a lesson in what is wrong with that unfortunate reasoning, recall how *sceptical* reasoning proceeds. For instance, the Cartesian dreaming argument says that your apparently observational data about the physical world *could* be due to your dreaming. So, different interpretations of these data are *possible*: (i) you are seeing the world; (ii) you are dreaming (your seeing) the world. The sceptical reasoning infers, from the possibility of this choice, your *not knowing* the physical world. But the idea of fallible knowledge allows us to be *non*-sceptical, by conceding the triviality that you know the physical world *fallibly*. And now (with that classic piece of epistemology in hand) return to the history case. We may say that we *do* know of the Jewish Holocaust's occurring in World War II – even if there is a slight fallibility within that knowledge. The key word here is 'slight'. It is the most that need be conceded. And it denotes only a philosophical technicality, not a substantive concern: your knowledge that you are sitting down is *also* slightly fallible, in that same merely technical sense. In this way, therefore, the no-mass-killings-in-gas-chambers interpretation functions like a purely sceptical possibility. It is no more sensible than that! Even if all historical knowledge is fallible, at its strongest (such as in our knowing of the Holocaust's having occurred!) it is only *slightly* fallible – in a technical sense that *allows it still to be knowledge.* This is what all historical knowledge is like – as indeed is all knowledge of the physical world.

6.4.3 Society

Question. 'As an individual, I learn so much through being accepted by, and accepting of, other people – what they say or write. When my surrounding society – my cultural environment – adopts a view, it is most likely correct: I should treat it as knowledge. Ultimately, knowing is socially constituted and constrained. Society is the highest authority that I can consult when seeking knowledge.' Is this so?

Society: argument. Our concepts and language are due to our being raised socially. As adults, we continue relying on others for knowledge. We trust socially organized and approved groups and institutions. As we should do: when people have maintained an orderly and cohesive society, this is great evidence of their generating and using knowledge. So many people agreeing with each other could not easily be wrong.

Society: counter-argument. In epistemic terms, there are different sorts of society. Some care more deeply about truth than others do. Some welcome challenging new ideas; some do not. Some are open to real inquiry, no matter where it might lead; not all are. Here we meet aspects of the difference between what Karl Popper called *closed* societies and *open* societies.

- A closed society can be culturally cohesive, bonding around its members' shared traditions of behaviour and belief. But such a society has significant *epistemic* limitations. It is not open to questioning those traditions: members accept as true whatever beliefs they have in their role *as* members of the society. ('Those beliefs define us. They make us who we are.') Can mistaken beliefs be replaced by more accurate ones within a closed society? Perhaps, but it is less likely to occur.
- An open society is different in that respect: it is always open to new beliefs, including central ones. In general, its members recognize that even long-treasured beliefs can be false. New beliefs might replace falsity with truth. This replacement can proceed in knowledge-producing ways. How does that happen? By being open to new ideas, and to testing them fairly. By *proposing* hypotheses, interpretations, ideas; by subjecting these to rational *testing*. This can involve such intellectual virtues as genuinely caring about truth and being receptive to the real possibility of having been mistaken.

We may use the term 'society' broadly. North Korea is currently a closed society. It is politically and therefore epistemically closed: its political realities restrict what truths reach its citizens. But we should not presume that all is open within 'the Western world': some political parties and religions, for example, are quite closed, even within countries that are open in many respects. Think of how rigidly such groups can depend on assumptions about what is true and what may appropriately be believed – with no dissent being tolerated. Penalties for dissent can range from formal expulsion to social exclusion.

Strikingly, we now live with easy access to potentially the most epistemically open society of all – the internet. (At least we do while it is uncontrolled by restrictive governmental or commercial interests.) Of course, this epistemic openness – such strong access to knowledge – brings epistemic risks, real possibilities of being fooled into thinking that one is gaining knowledge when in fact one is not. (Fake news?) How do you know which sites to *trust*, among whatever you find online? You do *not* automatically know this. Learning to use the internet wisely, so as to gain knowledge reliably, is like learning your way around a new social setting. Be alert for signs of falsity. You might treat sites like hypotheses, with few if any barriers having impeded their being proposed (posted) online. Test them, looking for evidence of falsity or unreliability. Seek the key elements of knowing – truth, and good evidence.

Never forget, too, how people within one society can react with widespread scorn, even horror, to something regarded by another society as unquestionably known. For example, compare our shared view on the moral abomination of human slavery with the usual view on it, at least among those in power, within the ancient world, such as in Athens when and where Western philosophy was being born. Do we know – by looking to *our* social norms – that slavery is immoral? We hope that we do. It is almost impossible for us to imagine that it is not. But must we find *more* than social agreement, if we are to know slavery's wrongness? Agreement with our own favoured social grouping is not agreement with *all* social groupings that have had views on this. So, we need to continue thinking, looking for evidence *beyond* mere social agreement, if we are genuinely to know what we think we know. We need *better* evidence than that social agreement as such.

6.4.4 Science

Question. 'One important social setting is the world of science, especially as we seek to know the world's underlying details. If we are cautious about regarding even some well-ordered societies as sources of knowledge, should we also be cautious about accepting what scientists say? Is the world of science sufficiently well ordered to be giving us knowledge? Scientists are fallible; they disagree with each other; and scientific theories are just that – theories. Must we believe them, at least on 'big' issues?' Does science give us knowledge, especially 'big' knowledge?

Science: argument. For example, currently almost all relevant scientists say that the world is undergoing global climate change caused to a significant extent by humans. Yet even here there is disagreement. Some *dissenters* are scientists. Should they be believed? It can be difficult to know. But they should make us more cautious: we should not automatically believe people called 'scientists'. Like people in other professions, scientists can succumb to intellectual fashion and to what George Orwell (in his novel *Nineteen Eighty-Four*, mentioned in section 3.2) famously called 'groupthink'. Hence, not all scientists need always be believed. Even 'official' science has made mistakes (including 'big' ones), and will continue doing so. Bear in mind, too, how much scientific research is funded by companies with substantial financial interests in the research's outcome. This compromises the research's epistemic integrity, weakening the quality of the evidence provided by the research. (Is such research really only 'research' – apparent research, not real research?) Too often, therefore, scientific research is not producing a well enough (scientifically) justified true belief. Too often, therefore, it is not producing (scientific) knowledge.

Science: counter-argument. When working well, scientists constitute an *open* society (in the sense mentioned in section 6.4.3): they answer to each other professionally when proposing and testing theories; they might well relinquish theories in the face of counter-evidence. Disagreeing with each other does not automatically deny them knowledge. Disagreeing can even be a step *towards* knowing. Disagreeing might mean only that a scientific process is under way; scientific knowledge could still emerge – even if it will be fallible knowledge. Scientific knowledge can arise from scientists taking risks. Good scientists are open to new ideas, hence to making new mistakes. No matter: science's history gives us inductive evidence that, overall, science succeeds, often *enough*. Science uncovers much truth, even if fallibly, and even while making mistakes along the way. Science has been essential to uncovering so many truths that have been vital to social development. Often, this happens collaboratively, across different countries – which can generate mistakes. But how are those mistakes discovered? By doing *more* science. Disagreement might exist within a group, as new ideas are discussed. Still, further tests can be run. At some point, a result might be reached that amounts to knowledge. It will have been collectively well justified, even if fallibly. Again, we need not be scared of that fallibility. It reflects how open the world's scientific society can be. Particularly in the long run, this is an epistemic strength within science's functioning properly. (By the way, a scientific result's being a *theory* does not prevent its being knowledge. Theories can be true. They can be well justified. Perhaps later evidence will cast doubt on a particular theory's being true; perhaps a better theory will take its place. Or perhaps not. All of this implies the importance of holding a theory in a properly inquiring way. We can hold it non-dogmatically. We would remain open to improving it, even to replacing it, as part of being intellectually virtuous inquirers. In practice, we *might* never need to improve the theory. In the meantime, we could continue using – testing – the theory. We would remain ready or poised to modify or discard it.)

6.5 Knowledge's value – again

Sections 6.2 through 6.4 show how thinking carefully about knowledge – doing epistemology – can sharpen our views on personally and socially significant questions.

This suggests that epistemology matters, perhaps greatly. For a start, it tells us that understanding knowledge can matter – because knowing can matter to so much else that matters.

Of course, this does not show that knowing *always* matters. Imagine that you are standing, for the first time, on an ocean beach. To some, it is a majestic sight. They admire the sounds and shapes of the water; they could feel dizzy from the unending sky. What do *you* do? You wonder, idly, how many grains of sand there are on the beach. This is indeed a possible object of knowledge. Yet it is unlikely to be important knowledge for you: it could seem trivial, even to you, and let us suppose that it will never give you any deep insight into … well, anything. (No inspiring mathematical result will flow from it for you.)

Still, it can be humanly vital to have specific knowledge. In sections 6.2 through 6.4, we discussed several kinds of case like that – self-knowledge, moral-knowledge, world-knowledge. Now imagine, more pressingly, being in a war zone. You encounter a bomb that needs – really needs – to be defused. By you! How much time do you have for doing this? You want – you need – to know. Nothing less will do, you feel. Annihilation looms for a village if you cannot defuse the bomb. This *should* matter to you. It *does* matter to you. (And five minutes are available for the defusing, by the way.)

What is the relevant difference between those two experiential situations – the beach and the bomb? First compare *what* is being known: in general, knowing the number of sand-grains on a beach is less important to people than is knowing how much time is available for defusing a bomb. Why is that so? Here, we might remember section 3.8: maybe the difference in general importance reflects what can usually be *done* with the knowledge in question. That is, the importance of having knowledge is a matter of possible *actions* – how the specific knowledge can be *used*. In general, having knowledge matters if we can *use* it in ways that themselves matter to us.

This idea need not be interpreted, narrowly, as the knowledge's being able to be used in a technical or money-making way. That is not all that matters to people. The idea is more general: for example, if some knowledge can help us to improve our thinking about the possibility of there being a God, this might matter. Let us not forget, by the way, what has been called 'the usefulness of useless knowledge'. Science's history, especially, includes many cases of knowledge that might initially have seemed useless – but that became vital in the creation of some of our shared lives' most practical elements, such as antibiotics and electricity.

Obviously, in using knowledge, what matters is not only *what* is being known. *How* is it being known? That also matters. For example, epistemology tells us that part of your knowing something could be your *having in mind good evidence* for it. In which case, the knowing might matter because you can helpfully use – by citing and explaining – your evidence when questioned by other people. You thereby let those other people know that they can use you as a good informant, thanks to your being someone who knows. Your knowing can thus be socially helpful. And your evidence might alert you to other facts, related ones. It could be socially or personally important for you to be aware of these, depending on the situation.

Can knowing also be *inherently* valuable – 'there is something special about being in a state of knowing!' – rather than valuable just through what useful actions it could generate? The virtue-epistemological view of knowledge (section 4.5.4) might say so. Suppose that knowing something involves forming a belief in an intellectually virtuous way, such as by inquiring open-mindedly while genuinely seeking truth. Then knowing includes having a *personal capacity* to act in that way. One has a personal quality *reflected* in one's knowing. And it is a personal quality that we might regard as part of being *a better person* – no matter what, if any, actions it ever generates. Could this be inherently valuable for a person – her being better simply *as* a person, considered apart from what actions, if ever, she ever performs as a result?

6.6 Knowing, knowledge-how, and pragmatism

In any event, to whatever extent it is that knowing's importance is the importance of its potential uses, this seems to make knowing-*how* important.

We imagined your knowing that there are five minutes available for defusing that bomb. We asked whether this knowledge matters because of how you can use it. This would mean your using the knowledge knowledgeably, not randomly. Having this capacity enables you to work effectively within those brief five minutes. But notice that your *knowledgeably using* that knowledge ('I have five minutes in which to do this' – you concentrate accordingly, as you start working) is your putting into effect some knowledge-*how*. You know that you have five minutes available. Yet this knowledge does not simply sit there – inert, as an end in itself – within your mind. As we are now imagining, you also know *how to use* this knowledge (of there being five minutes available): you know how to use it as it should be used. This analysis of the situation gives your knowledge a point – even a power – for you.

That description should remind us of the distinction (in section 2.4.2) between knowledge-*that* (this being what epistemologists typically designate with the word 'knowledge') and knowledge-*how* (knowing how to do something). We should now wonder whether knowing – knowing-that – matters, when it does, *because* of associated knowledge-how. When we seek knowledge (knowledge-that, knowledge of a fact), often we expect that having the knowledge will matter. Should we understand this as our rightly seeking the knowledge in order to *do* useful things with it? Is knowing important, whenever it is, because it gives us knowledge-how – a power or capacity enabling us to act knowledgeably?

If we say 'yes' to those questions, we are moving towards a *pragmatist* view of knowing's value. Pragmatism *per se* is a general style of philosophical thinking. One can be a philosophical pragmatist about many things – about morality, beauty, language, etc. To be a pragmatist in one's philosophical description of X is to say that an understanding of X need only talk about practical matters, if it is to adequately describe X philosophically. So, one can be a pragmatist about knowledge in at least two respects – about knowing's *value* (one instance of 'X'), and about what knowing *is* (another instance of 'X'). A pragmatist about part of knowledge's nature, for example, might say that part of what it *is* to know something is *to be able to act usefully* with the knowledge.

I have suggested a weaker pragmatist idea – that at least part of the *value* in knowing is the capacity or power to act usefully with the knowledge. On this picture, knowing – when valuable – enables us to act so as to *guide* our lives (and perhaps others' lives) in important ways. We would act knowledgeably, hopefully to benefit ourselves and others. This would be the value in knowing, whenever it has value. One could move accurately into new positions within reality – finding new places for one's body to wander. One could think accurately 'into' new ideas – finding new places for one's mind to wander. One could move from here to there, doing this or that – all accurately, thanks to the knowledge guiding one's movements. This usefulness might, but need not, be social, by helping others. It could be entirely one's own, enriching one's path through life. That is still usefulness, even if only for oneself.

6.7 Putting our theory of knowledge into action

I will end the book with some general advice on *how* to link knowledge with action. These suggestions hearken back to details within our working theory of knowledge. You could think of the following as practical ideas to hold in mind when seeking knowledge.

- Always be aware that you might be overlooking significant truths. Stay open-minded and alert to the possibility of needing further evidence if you are to have knowledge.
- Always be aware that you might be accepting significant falsehoods as truths. Stay open-minded and alert to the possibility of needing to discard some of your evidence if you are to have knowledge.
- Always be aware that, even when your evidence is leading you in one direction, it might be *mis*leading you. Stay open-minded and alert to the possibility of meeting – and welcoming – a new pattern of evidence if you are to have knowledge.
- Never fear fallibility as such, in yourself or others. Do not dismiss anyone as not knowing, simply because there is fallibility in their thinking. Rather, think hard about *how much* fallibility there is in their thinking. If it is not *too* much, then fallible knowledge might be present. It could be realistically strong – even if not literally unimprovable and thus perfect – knowledge.
- Never settle for needless fallibility, in yourself or others. Dig deeper, if this is realistic and helpful. Sometimes, deeper – fuller – knowledge of a fact is

also more practically useful than shallower knowledge of it.

Is there a recurring theme here? Yes. Stay open-
minded and alert, seeking the fullest and most accurate
significant evidence that is realistically and helpfully
available, when knowledge is at stake.
Keep It Knowledgeable.
Keep It Epistemological.

Further Reading

Chapter 1 Doing Epistemology

The book began by talking about what it is to be doing philosophy. The nature of philosophy can still puzzle philosophers. You might start with Bertrand Russell's classic, *The Problems of Philosophy* (London: Oxford University Press, 1959 [1912]), chapter XV. He sees philosophy as partly a process of *questioning*, as this book does. Philosophy can also involve the *analysing of concepts*: see P.F. Strawson's *Analysis and Metaphysics: An Introduction to Philosophy* (Oxford: Oxford University Press, 1992), chapter 1. For the distinction between the manifest image and the scientific image, see Wilfrid Sellars's 'Philosophy and the scientific image of man', chapter 1 of his *Science, Perception and Reality* (London: Routledge & Kegan Paul, 1963).

The chapter compares philosophy and religion in some respects. On actual and potential links between philosophy of religion and religious studies, see Thomas A. Lewis's *Why Philosophy Matters for the Study of Religion – and Vice Versa* (New York: Oxford University

Press, 2015). The chapter ends by hinting at epistemology's extensive history. For fuller senses of that history, see Robert Pasnau's *After Certainty: A History of Our Epistemic Ideals and Illusions* (Oxford: Oxford University Press, 2017), Stephen Hetherington (general editor) *The Philosophy of Knowledge: A History*, 4 vols. (London: Bloomsbury, 2019), and Stephen Hetherington (ed.), *Epistemology: The Key Thinkers*, 2nd edn. (London: Bloomsbury, 2019). Like those books, this one is on Western epistemology. But Western philosophers are starting to attend to Chinese epistemology: see, for example, Stephen Hetherington and Karyn Lai's 'Practising to know: Practicalism and Confucian philosophy', *Philosophy* 87 (2012), 375–93, and Barry Allen's *Vanishing into Things: Knowledge in Chinese Tradition* (Cambridge, MA: Harvard University Press, 2015).

Chapter 2 Kinds of Knowledge

This chapter gestures at many philosophical ideas about forms that can be taken by knowledge.

For the idea of an extended mind, see Andy Clark and David Chalmers's 'The extended mind', *Analysis* 58 (1998), 7–19, and, more recently, Clark's *Supersizing the Mind: Embodiment, Action, and Cognitive Extension* (New York: Oxford University Press, 2008). For Karl Popper's conception of objective knowledge, see his *Objective Knowledge: An Evolutionary Approach* (Oxford: Clarendon Press, 1972). On group knowledge, see Jon Hardwig's 'Epistemic dependence', *Journal of Philosophy* 82 (1985), 335–49, and Jennifer Lackey (ed.), *Essays in Collective Epistemology* (Oxford: Oxford University Press, 2014). On knowledge being possessed by animals, see Hilary Kornblith's *Knowledge and Its Place in Nature* (Oxford: Clarendon Press, 2002), chapter 2.

There is a vast literature on general ways to gain knowledge. Here are some of those readings:

- On perception, see Jonathan Dancy (ed.), *Perceptual Knowledge* (Oxford: Oxford University Press, 1988), Colin McGinn's *Inborn Knowledge: The Mystery Within* (Cambridge, MA: MIT Press, 2015), and Ali Hasan's *A Critical Introduction to the Epistemology of Perception* (London: Bloomsbury, 2017).
- On reason, see Paul K. Moser (ed.), *A Priori Knowledge* (New York: Oxford University Press, 1987), and Laurence BonJour's *In Defense of Pure Reason* (Cambridge: Cambridge University Press, 1998)
- On memory, see Bertrand Russell's *The Analysis of Mind* (London: George Allen & Unwin, 1921), lecture IX, and Thomas Senor's *A Critical Introduction to the Epistemology of Memory* (London: Bloomsbury, forthcoming).
- On testimony, see C.A.J. Coady's *Testimony: A Philosophical Study* (Oxford: Clarendon Press, 1992), Jennifer Lackey's *Learning from Words: Testimony as a Source of Knowledge* (Oxford: Oxford University Press, 2008), and Axel Gelfert's *A Critical Introduction to Testimony* (London: Bloomsbury, 2014).
- On introspection, see Andre Gallois's *The Word Without, The Mind Within* (Cambridge: Cambridge University Press, 1996), and Declan Smithies and Daniel Stoljar (eds.), *Introspection and Consciousness* (New York: Oxford University Press, 2012).
- On common sense, see G.E. Moore's 1925 'A defence of common sense', in his *Philosophical Papers* (London: George Allen & Unwin, 1959), and Noah Lemos's *Common Sense: A Contemporary Defense* (Cambridge: Cambridge University Press, 2004).
- On intuition, see Michal DePaul and William Ramsey (eds.), *Rethinking Intuition: The Psychology of Intuition and its Role in Philosophical Inquiry* (Lanham, MD: Rowman & Littlefield, 1998), and Elijah

Chudnoff's *Intuition* (Oxford: Oxford University Press, 2013).
* On knowing-what-it-is-like, see L.A. Paul's *Transformative Experience* (Oxford: Oxford University Press, 2014).

Running throughout the chapter's discussion is Bertrand Russell's evocative distinction between knowledge by description and knowledge by acquaintance: see *The Problems of Philosophy* (above), chapter V.

The chapter mentions knowing this rather than that – inherently *contrastive* knowledge. On the idea of such knowledge, see Jonathan Schaffer's 'From contextualism to contrastivism', *Philosophical Studies* 119 (2004), 73–104, and Martijn Blaauw (ed.), *Contrastivism in Philosophy* (New York: Routledge, 2012).

The chapter also mentions knowledge-how. Here, epistemologists look first to some of Gilbert Ryle's writing: see his 1946 'Knowing how and knowing that', in his *Collected Papers*, vol. II (London: Hutchinson, 1971), and *The Concept of Mind* (London: Hutchinson, 1949), chapter II. See also Jason Stanley and Timothy Williamson's 'Knowing how', *Journal of Philosophy* 98 (2001), 411–44, Stephen Hetherington's *How to Know: A Practicalist Conception of Knowledge* (Malden, MA: Wiley-Blackwell, 2011), chapter 2, John Bengson and Marc Moffett (eds.), *Knowing How: Essays on Knowledge, Mind, and Action* (New York: Oxford University Press, 2011), and J. Adam Carter and Ted Poston's *A Critical Introduction to Knowledge-How* (London: Bloomsbury, 2018).

Chapter 3 A First Theory of Knowledge

Central to this chapter are two discussions by Plato. See his *Meno*, at 97a–98d, and his *Theaetetus*, at 201c–210b. For commentary on the *Theaetetus*, see F.M.

Cornford's *Plato's Theory of Knowledge* (London: Routledge & Kegan Paul, 1935), John McDowell's *Plato's* Theaetetus (Oxford: Clarendon Press, 1973), and David Bostock's *Plato's* Theaetetus (Oxford: Clarendon Press, 1988). For commentary on the *Meno*, see R.S. Bluck's *Plato's* Meno (Cambridge: Cambridge University Press, 1961), and Dominic Scott's *Plato's* Meno (Cambridge: Cambridge University Press, 2006).

The third chapter takes us through a process of constructing carefully, step by step, a theory of knowledge. For a theory of knowledge as simply true belief, see Crispin Sartwell's 'Knowledge is merely true belief', *American Philosophical Quarterly* 28 (1991), 157–65, and 'Why knowledge is merely true belief', *Journal of Philosophy* 89 (1992), 167–80, as well as Richard Foley's *When Is True Belief Knowledge?* (Princeton: Princeton University Press, 2012). For some influential versions of the justified-true-belief analysis, see A.J. Ayer's *The Problem of Knowledge* (London: Macmillan, 1956), and any of the three editions of Roderick M. Chisholm's *Theory of Knowledge* (Englewood Cliffs, NJ: Prentice-Hall, 1966/1977/1989).

Knowledge's supposed components are highlighted independently within the chapter:

- On truth, see Richard L. Kirkham's *Theories of Truth: A Critical Introduction* (Cambridge, MA: The MIT Press, 1992), and Simon Blackburn and Keith Simmons (eds.), *Truth* (Oxford: Oxford University Press, 1999).
- On belief, see L. Jonathan Cohen's *An Essay on Belief and Acceptance* (Oxford: Clarendon Press, 1992), and Aaron Z. Zimmerman's *Belief: A Pragmatic Picture* (Oxford: Oxford University Press, 2018).
- On epistemic justification, see Alvin Goldman's 'What is justified belief?', in George S. Pappas (ed.), *Justification and Knowledge: New Studies in Epistemology* (Dordrecht: D. Reidel, 1979), and Laurence BonJour

and Ernest Sosa's *Epistemic Justification: Internalism vs. Externalism, Foundations vs. Virtues* (Malden, MA: Blackwell, 2003).

For the ESP kind of example, see Laurence BonJour's *The Structure of Empirical Knowledge* (Cambridge, MA: Harvard University Press, 1985), chapter 3. On the historical importance within philosophy of the idea of an explanatory principle, mentioned in this chapter as able to be part of a *logos*, see Peter Anstey's 'A very principled project', *Humanities Australia* 8 (2017), 80–5.

The chapter asks about the relationship between knowledge and understanding. See Jonathan L. Kvanvig's *The Value of Knowledge and the Pursuit of Understanding* (Cambridge: Cambridge University Press, 2003), Catherine Z. Elgin's *True Enough* (Cambridge, MA: MIT Press, 2017), and Stephen R. Grimm, Christoph Baumberger, and Sabine Ammon (eds.), *Explaining Understanding: New Perspectives from Epistemology and Philosophy of Science* (New York: Routledge, 2017).

Chapter 4 Refining Our Theory of Knowledge

Bertrand Russell's stopped-clock case is from *Human Knowledge: Its Scope and Limits* (London: George Allen & Unwin, 1948), pp. 170–1. Edmund Gettier's famous article is 'Is justified true belief knowledge?' *Analysis* 23 (1963), 121–3. For the initial version of the sheep-in-the-field case, see the first edition of Roderick Chisholm's *Theory of Knowledge* (Englewood Cliffs, NJ: Prentice-Hall, 1966), p. 23n22. For an excellent collection of articles from post-Gettier epistemology, see George S. Pappas and Marshall Swain (eds.), *Essays on Knowledge and Justification* (Ithaca, NY: Cornell University Press, 1978). That book includes the fake-barns

case, in Alvin Goldman's 'Discrimination and perceptual knowledge', plus the idea of a defeater, along with
a defeasibility view of knowledge, in Keith Lehrer and
Thomas D. Paxson's 'Knowledge: Undefeated justified
true belief'.

On virtue epistemology, see Linda T. Zagzebski's
*Virtues of the Mind: An Inquiry Into the Nature of
Virtue and the Ethical Foundations of Knowledge*
(Cambridge: Cambridge University Press, 1996), Robert
C. Roberts and W. Jay Wood's *Intellectual Virtues: An
Essay in Regulative Epistemology* (Oxford: Clarendon
Press, 2007), Ernest Sosa's *A Virtue Epistemology: Apt
Belief and Reflective Knowledge*, Vol. I (Oxford: Clar-
endon Press, 2007), and John Greco's *Achieving Know-
ledge: A Virtue-Theoretic Account of Epistemic
Normativity* (Cambridge: Cambridge University Press,
2010). On intellectual vices, see Charlie Crerar's 'Moti-
vational approaches to intellectual vice', *Australasian
Journal of Philosophy* 96 (2018), 753–66.

For surveys of post-Gettier epistemology, see Robert
K. Shope's *The Analysis of Knowing: A Decade of
Research* (Princeton: Princeton University Press, 1983),
Stephen Hetherington's 'Gettier problem', in *Rout-
ledge Encyclopedia of Philosophy* (2016), at https://
www.rep.routledge.com/articles/thematic/gettier-
problems/v-2, and Stephen Hetherington (ed.), *The
Gettier Problem* (Cambridge: Cambridge University
Press, 2018). For critical discussion of post-Gettier epis-
temology, see Stephen Hetherington's *Knowledge and
the Gettier Problem* (Cambridge: Cambridge University
Press, 2016).

Experimental epistemology entered philosophy with
Jonathan Weinberg, Shaun Nichols, and Stephen Stich's
'Normativity and epistemic intuitions', *Philosophical
Topics* 29 (2001), 429–60. On the role of intuition within
philosophy, see Herman Cappelen's *Philosophy without
Intuitions* (Oxford: Oxford University Press, 2012). For
critical discussion of experimental philosophy, see Max

Deutsch's *The Myth of the Intuitive: Experimental Philosophy and Philosophical Method* (Cambridge, MA: MIT Press, 2015).

Knowledge-first epistemology entered contemporary philosophy with Timothy Williamson's *Knowledge and Its Limits* (Oxford: Clarendon Press, 2000). For discussion, see Aidan McGlynn's *Knowledge First?* (Basingstoke: Palgrave Macmillan, 2014). On knowledge and action, see John Hawthorne and Jason Stanley's 'Knowledge and action', *Journal of Philosophy* 105 (2008), 571–90, and Stephen Hetherington's 'Knowledge as potential for action', *European Journal of Pragmatism and American Philosophy* 9/2 (2017), at http://journals.openedition.org/ejpap/1070.

Chapter 5 Is It Even Possible to Have Knowledge?

Both the dreaming argument and the evil demon argument appear in René Descartes's 'Meditation I', in his *Meditations on First Philosophy* (1641). The *Cogito* is in his 'Meditation II'. The two main translations of these are by E.S. Haldane and G.R.T. Ross, *The Philosophical Works of Descartes*, Vol. I (Cambridge: Cambridge University Press, 1911), and by J. Cottingham, R. Stoothoff, and D. Murdoch, *The Philosophical Writings of Descartes*, Vol. II (Cambridge: Cambridge University Press, 1984). On Descartes's dreaming argument, see Barry Stroud's *The Significance of Philosophical Scepticism* (Oxford: Clarendon Press, 1984), chapter 1, Ernest Sosa's *A Virtue Epistemology: Apt Belief and Reflective Knowledge*, Vol. I (Oxford: Clarendon Press, 2007), chapter 1, and Allan Hazlett's *A Critical Introduction to Skepticism* (London: Bloomsbury, 2014), chapter 4.

For brain-in-a-vat scepticism, see Hilary Putnam's *Reason, Truth and History* (Cambridge: Cambridge University Press, 1981), chapter 1. For discussion (also of Descartes's argument), see Keith DeRose and Ted A.

Warfield (eds.), *Skepticism: A Contemporary Reader* (New York: Oxford University Press, 1999).

On the general form of sceptical reasoning, see A.J. Ayer's *The Problem of Knowledge* (London: Macmillan, 1956), pp. 81–7. For a classic common-sense reply to external world scepticism, see G.E. Moore's 1939 'Proof of an external world', in his *Philosophical Papers* (London: George Allen & Unwin, 1959). On intuitions, see the readings suggested above, for chapter 4, on experimental philosophy.

For David Hume's inductive scepticism (as it is now called), see section IV of his *Enquiry Concerning Human Understanding* (1748). The second edition of that book was edited by L.A. Selby-Bigge (Oxford: Clarendon Press, 1902). For two enlightening discussions of Hume, see Stephen Buckle's *Hume's Enlightenment Tract: The Unity and Purpose of* An Enquiry Concerning Human Understanding (Oxford: Clarendon Press, 2001), Part 2, Section IV, and Don Garrett's *Hume* (New York: Routledge, 2015), chapter 7.

On other minds scepticism, see Anita Avramides's *Other Minds* (London: Routledge, 2001). For a classic reply – the argument from analogy – to such scepticism, see John Stuart Mill's *An Examination of Sir William Hamilton's Philosophy* (1865), chapter XII.

For introspection scepticism, via the discussion of linguistic rule-following and associated doubts about whether a 'private language' is possible, see Ludwig Wittgenstein's *Philosophical Investigations* (Oxford: Blackwell, 1953), sections 1–88, 143–242, and Saul A. Kripke's *Wittgenstein on Rules and Private Language: An Elementary Exposition* (Cambridge, MA: Harvard University Press, 1982).

On the possibility of the world's having begun only five minutes ago, see Bertrand Russell's *The Analysis of Mind* (London: George Allen & Unwin, 1921), lecture IX. For discussion, see Thomas Baldwin's 'Russell on memory', *Principia* 5 (2001), 187–208.

On the epistemology of disagreement, see Richard Feldman's 'Epistemological puzzles about disagreement', in Stephen Hetherington (ed.), *Epistemology Futures* (Oxford: Clarendon Press, 2006), Richard Feldman and Ted A. Warfield (eds.), *Disagreement* (Oxford: Oxford University Press, 2010), and Allan Hazlett's *A Critical Introduction to Skepticism* (London: Bloomsbury, 2014), chapter 2.

For the zebras-vs-disguised mules sceptical possibility, see Fred Dretske's 'Epistemic operators', *Journal of Philosophy* 67: 1007–23. On contextualism and sceptical thinking, see Michael Williams's *Unnatural Doubts: Epistemological Realism and the Basis of Scepticism* (Oxford: Blackwell, 1991), David Lewis's 'Elusive knowledge', *Australasian Journal of Philosophy* 74 (1996), 549–67, and Keith DeRose's 'Contextualism: An explanation and defense', in John Greco and Ernest Sosa (eds.), *The Blackwell Guide to Epistemology* (Malden, MA: Blackwell, 1999). For an overview, see Michael Blome-Tillmann's 'Knowledge as contextual', in Stephen Hetherington and Markos Valaris (eds.), *Knowledge in Contemporary Philosophy* (London: Bloomsbury, 2019).

On fallibility and knowledge, see Stephen Hetherington's 'Fallibilism', *Internet Encyclopedia of Philosophy*, at http://www.iep.utm.edu/f/fallibil.htm (2005), and 'Knowing failably', *Journal of Philosophy* 96 (1999), 565–87, along with Trent Dougherty's 'Fallibilism', in Sven Bernecker and Duncan Pritchard (eds.), *The Routledge Companion to Epistemology* (New York: Routledge, 2011). On knowing a fact by 'burrowing into' it more – or less – deeply, see Stephen Hetherington's *How to Know: A Practicalist Conception of Knowledge* (Malden, MA: Wiley Blackwell, 2011), chapter 5.

On epistemic levels, see William P. Alston's 'Level confusions in epistemology', in his *Epistemic Justification: Essays in the Theory of Knowledge* (Ithaca, NY: Cornell University Press, 1989). On the KK-principle, the classic analysis is Jaakko Hintikka's, in his *Knowledge and Belief: An Introduction to the Logic of the Two Notions* (Ithaca, NY: Cornell University Press, 1962), chapter 5. But his book is quite technical. There has been no informal and similarly detailed discussion of the KK principle. For some discussion of the principle and Hintikka's account, see E.J. Lemmon's 'If I know, do I know that I know?', in Avrum Stroll (ed.), *Epistemology: New Essays in the Theory of Knowledge* (New York: Harper & Row, 1967). For the distinction between animal knowledge and reflective knowledge, see Ernest Sosa's *Reflective Knowledge: Apt Belief and Reflective Knowledge*, Vol. II (Oxford: Clarendon Press, 2009), chapter 7.

For an excellent survey of scepticism, including its history, see Diego E. Machuca and Baron Reed (eds.), *Skepticism: From Antiquity to the Present* (London: Bloomsbury, 2018).

Chapter 6 Applying Epistemology

Epistemologists do not publish much on how to apply their abstract theories to practical questions. An accessible exception is David Coady's *What To Believe Now: Applying Epistemology to Contemporary Issues* (Malden, MA: Wiley-Blackwell, 2012). A more difficult exception is Alvin Goldman's *Knowledge in a Social World* (Oxford: Clarendon Press, 1999). See also Harvey Siegel's *Education's Epistemology: Rationality, Diversity, and Critical Thinking* (New York: Oxford University Press, 2017). For some applied epistemology criticizing various key elements of traditional epistemology, see Michael A. Bishop and J.D. Trout's *Epistemology and the Psychology of Human Judgment* (New York: Oxford University Press, 2005).

For the general categories of question in this chapter, here are some relevant readings.

On self-knowledge, see Stephen Hetherington's *Self-Knowledge: Beginning Philosophy Right Here and Now* (Peterborough, Ontario: Broadview Press, 2007), Brie Gertler's *Self-Knowledge* (Abingdon: Routledge, 2011), Quassim Cassam's *Self-Knowledge for Humans* (Oxford: Oxford University Press, 2014), and L.A. Paul's *Transformative Experience* (Oxford: Oxford University Press, 2014).

On moral-knowledge, see Alan H. Goldman's *Moral Knowledge* (London: Routledge, 1988), Walter Sinnott-Armstrong and Mark Timmons (eds.), *Moral Knowledge? New Readings in Moral Epistemology* (New York: Oxford University Press, 1996), and Michael Huemer's *Ethical Intuitionism* (Basingstoke: Palgrave Macmillan, 2005). There is increasing interest in how questions about social privilege and prejudice interact with questions about epistemic matters. Some of this interest is sparked by Miranda Fricker's *Epistemic Injustice: Power and the Ethics of Knowing* (Oxford: Oxford University Press, 2007). See also Axel Gelfert's *A Critical Introduction to Testimony* (London: Bloomsbury, 2014), chapter 10. The question about the death penalty concerns how reliably criminal trials lead to truth and knowledge. On such matters, see Larry Laudan's *Truth, Error and Criminal Law: An Essay in Legal Epistemology* (Cambridge: Cambridge University Press, 2006).

On the epistemology of history, see Stephen R. Grimm's 'Why study history? On its epistemic benefits and its relation to the sciences', *Philosophy* 92 (2017), 399–420. For Karl Popper's distinction between open societies and closed societies, see his *The Open Society and Its Enemies*, Vol. I: *The Spell of Plato*, 5th edn. (London: Routledge, 1966 [1945]). On attempts to explain away the use of gas chambers to kill Jews, see Deborah Lipstadt's *Denying the Holocaust: The Growing Assault on Truth and Memory* (London: Penguin, 1993), chapter 9.

On knowledge of God, see William P. Alston's *Perceiving God: The Epistemology of Religious Experience* (Ithaca, NY: Cornell University Press, 1991), Alvin Plantinga's *Warranted Christian Belief* (New York: Oxford University Press, 2000), Michael L. Peterson and Raymond J. VanArragon (eds.), *Contemporary Debates in Philosophy of Religion* (Malden, MA: Blackwell, 2004), Parts I and II, and Linda T. Zagzebski's *The Philosophy of Religion: An Historical Introduction* (Malden, MA: Blackwell, 2007), chapters 1–3. On the idea of any actual world's automatically being orderly (even if not created), see Nicholas Rescher's *Nature and Understanding: The Metaphysics and Method of Science* (Oxford: Clarendon Press, 2000), chapter 8. On whether this world must have been caused by a necessarily existing being, such as a God, see Alexander Pruss and Joshua Rasmussen's *Necessary Existence* (New York: Oxford University Press, 2018), chapter 3. For Plato's argument against an action's moral goodness *being* its being approved of by a God, see his *Euthyphro*, at 9e–11b.

On scientific theories, see Peter Godfrey-Smith's *Theory and Reality: An Introduction to the Philosophy of Science* (Chicago, IL: University of Chicago Press, 2003). On science and fallibility, see Karl Popper's 'On the sources of knowledge and of ignorance', in his *Conjectures and Refutations: The Growth of Scientific Knowledge* (London: Routledge & Kegan Paul, 1963). The philosophy of science is an enormous area of study, and I cannot even begin to represent it adequately here. For one influential linking, though, of science with epistemology, see W.V. Quine's 'Epistemology naturalized', in his *Ontological Relativity and Other Essays* (New York: Columbia University Press, 1969). Another major source of questions for the epistemology of scientific thinking is Thomas S. Kuhn's *The Structure of Scientific Revolutions* (Chicago, IL: University of Chicago Press, 1962/1970/1996).

On the value of knowing, see Jonathan L. Kvanvig's *The Value of Knowledge and the Pursuit of Understanding* (Cambridge: Cambridge University Press, 2003) and Duncan Pritchard, Alan Millar, and Adrian Haddock's *The Nature and Value of Knowledge: Three Investigations* (Oxford: Oxford University Press, 2010). On the idea of useful useless knowledge, see Abraham Flexner's 'The usefulness of useless knowledge', *Journal of Chronic Diseases* 2 (1955), 241–6. (That paper now appears, with commentary by Robbert Dijkgraaf, as a 2017 Princeton University Press book of the same title.) For the link between knowing and being a good informant, see Edward Craig's *Knowledge and the State of Nature: An Essay in Conceptual Synthesis* (Oxford: Clarendon Press, 1990). For pragmatist conceptions of knowing, see C.I. Lewis's *An Analysis of Knowledge and Valuation* (La Salle, IL: Open Court, 1946) and Stephen Hetherington's 'Knowledge as potential for action', *European Journal of Pragmatism and American Philosophy* 9/2 (2017), at http://journals.openedition. org/ejpap/1070. For a pragmatism about belief's nature, see Aaron Zimmerman's *Belief: A Pragmatic Picture* (New York: Oxford University Press, 2018).

Finally, the chapter's parting advice – on the importance of attending to aspects of what it is to know, when inquiring – is inspired loosely by a classic moment in the history of epistemology: René Descartes's 1637 *Discourse on Method*, Part II. (See above, for the leading translations of his writings.) Descartes presents rules by which he sought to discipline his thinking, so as to ensure that he would be gaining knowledge, not simply accepting whatever his past habits and social authorities would have him believe. This is potentially admirable self-discipline. It involves being as epistemological as is realistically possible.